the last
ISLAND

For Kim

"In order to go on
it is necessary to go back."

Lawrence Durrell, *The Alexandria Quartet*

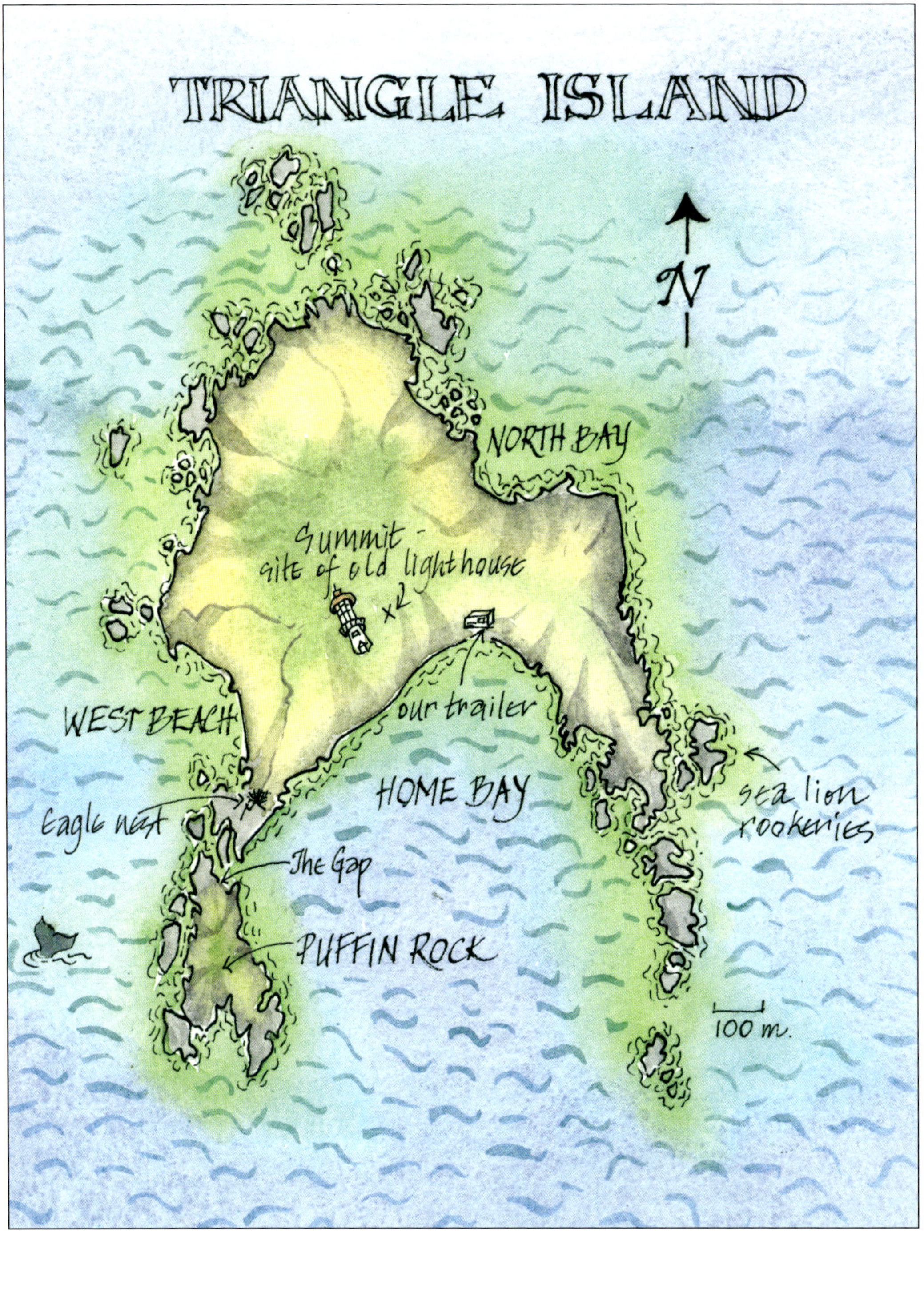
TRIANGLE ISLAND
N
NORTH BAY
Summit -
site of old lighthouse
x2
our trailer
WEST BEACH
HOME BAY
sea lion
rookeries
Eagle nest
The Gap
PUFFIN ROCK
100 m.

INTRODUCTION

August 15, 1996

I am falling upward—the ground dropping away so fast my stomach clenches. Suddenly it is as if no time has passed—I am twenty-three, not thirty-nine. Once again I have been seduced by a romantic notion of adventure, and, once again the moment of departure has filled me with disbelief—for some reason I have planned to fly off the edge of the world.

As we leave the long sand beach of Cape Scott behind, I imagine how we must look to the hikers who have set a yellow tent there—a helicopter growing smaller and smaller until it is a tiny speck, an insect that has lost its bearing and is flying inexplicably out to sea.

I lean on the cold glass of the window, to see the Scott Islands scattered below us, the first low and heavily wooded, like fragments of Vancouver Island unmoored and set adrift, the farthest rugged and treeless. Finally we seem to leave land behind.

"Flying out here, over nothing but water, makes me nervous," I confess to the pilot.

"Me too," he says, adjusting his headset and giving me a quick sideways glance and an incomprehensible smile.

The thrum of the blades makes conversation impossible. Their blur is mesmerizing. I'm gripped by a deep skepticism. How can they keep us aloft until we get there? Surely we are not meant to do this.

As if to reassure me, the pilot points. "There she is."

Thirty miles out, a dark shape hunches against the sky: Triangle Island, the last island.

As we get closer it resolves like a Polaroid: immense cliffs rise straight up from the sea. At their feet huge waves explode into white spray.

For a moment I'm stunned that this place is real. Over the years it has become imaginary—its remoteness transforming memory to dream. But it has been here all the time. While I was absorbed in sixteen years of my own life, the rituals of the island's seasons, the private lives of its creatures, were still unfolding.

Birds fly up from golden slopes in a dark swarm as we pass over the first ridge. Far below me is the long curve of a bay. Three

the last island

tiny figures stand in front of a cabin waving madly. The helicopter slows and drops, nimble as a dragonfly. A moment later we touch down and I step once more onto Triangle Island.

A woman runs toward us smiling. Her hair is light brown, a nest of tangled dreadlocks with bright cotton strands, beads and shells woven into it. She thrusts out her hand.

"Hi, I'm Laura."

A compact man striding energetically behind her introduces himself as Richard. His curly hair is pulled back into a ponytail; his luxuriant beard is dusted with crumbs of granola he's eating by the handful. He wears threadbare pants with wide tears at the knees and backside; his shoes are bound with duct tape. I feel too tidy, my clothes too clean and pressed, like a Victorian missionary meeting a jungle tribe.

They look past me, at the boxes of groceries the pilot is heaving out of the helicopter, grab them eagerly and hurry back to the cabin. I shoulder my pack and duffel bags and follow them along

the narrow terrace between cliffs and beach. I note the familiar signs explaining that Triangle Island is a seabird colony and restricted and am reminded why I am here—for the same reason I first came here—to study tufted puffins. With a shock I read a new sign: "Anne Vallée Ecological Reserve." A memory of the face of that lost friend, as I watched her waving from this shore, sweeps over me.

I shake myself and carry on to the cabin. To my relief it is not the decrepit structure I knew but a new aluminum frame covered with wallboard and siding. It faces the sea and is surrounded by cow parsley, stinging nettle, ferns, salmonberry, and stalks of figwort thick with bumblebees intently prying red flowers open.

A woman in her early twenties, like the other biologists here, emerges from the doorway. Her dark hair is loose around her shoulders.

"Welcome to Triangle Island," she says, "I'm Hannah." Her eyes light up when she sees the food.

"We ran out of fresh stuff two weeks ago," she says as if apologizing for dispensing with any more polite conversation. Darting toward Laura, she snatches a box from her, and begins rummaging through it, triumphantly holding up ripe tomatoes, basil, loaves of bread.

I step inside the cabin. It smells like curry and wet socks. I let my eyes adjust to the dimness, and look around. The main room has a table, a gas range and oven, a sink and shelves stacked with food. Hanging over a wood stove in the corner is a canopy of drying racks festooned with rain gear. On the wall closest to the sea are a window and a counter for working. The walls are crammed with shelves of reference books. I cross the narrow floor in three strides. The cabin seems impossibly small for all of us, yet I know that when the storms roll off the Pacific, finally finding some land to punish, we'll gratefully hurry to its warmth.

As I dump my gear on a musty bunk in a tiny bedroom, a sheaf of stapled papers drops out of my pack—the *Triangle Island Users Manual*, which I received from the Canadian Wildlife Service as part of my information package. It falls open on a page headed "Working on Triangle Island."

"You must be in good physical condition," I read, "to scramble up steep slopes and walk along rocky and slippery beaches. You must be able to live and work in a cramped isolated setting with others whose world-views differ from your own. You must be able to work odd hours."

At the bottom of the page it cautions: "Walk slowly and carefully and do not jump or make uncontrolled moves, particularly when crossing driftwood piles or algae covered rocks…watch sea conditions carefully when crossing wave washed areas such as the 'Gap' and be aware of the possibility of sudden unexpected 'rogue' waves…cliff edges on Triangle Island are usually concealed from view by grasses or other vegetation and thus pose an extreme hazard."

I peer through the tiny window at Triangle's cliffs—serene, indifferent. I return to the kitchen to find the others singing to a reggae CD, laughing and talking over their day while the cabin fills with pungent steam curling off the stove top. They are a family of sorts, brought together by the demands of the work and the place.

Over dinner they ask about Anne.

PART ONE

Part One

April 28, 1980

The pilot was eager to get back before the storm broke. He helped unload our gear as quickly as he could—tanks of propane, mist nets, plywood to construct blinds, tools, food—then climbed back into his seat. The engine whined into a roar, the long blades circling slowly at first, then quickening, the tempest of their wake whipping our hair around our faces. Hot exhaust flattened the grass. The helicopter rose and disappeared.

We stood for a moment in silence, looking around. I had never seen such a desolate place. Waves lashed snags of black rock; the land rose in steep folds, brown and treeless. At the summit, far above us, dark clouds hung like torn flags.

Anne turned to the supplies, and began carrying them to a tiny trailer. I chose a box marked "reference books." Shrubs tore at the skin of my hands as I pushed through the overgrown path. The trailer, white with mustard-yellow trim, was stained with nail rust. Strips of aluminum siding curled back as if someone had tried to pry them off. The door was wet and swollen and we had to dig our shoulders into it before it gave way. A musty odour rushed out. Inside, two windows facing the sea cast pale, wintry squares of light onto the gloom. Rough shelves framed the windows. At the far end of the room was an old airtight stove with a collapsed pipe. Beside it was a cupboard with a latched door, gnawed on the corners. The only furniture was a plywood table and a bench of driftwood planks nailed to log ends.

I leaned over the table to the window. The ledge was littered with dead flies. Lined up carefully were a delicate, sun-bleached bird skull, the white tail feather of a bald eagle and a turquoise egg etched with dark marks like hieroglyphics. I set down my books, rubbed a clear circle in the salt rime on the glass and peered through to the deserted beach beyond. A few steps away was the bedroom, just big enough for two bunk beds huddled against opposite walls. I pressed my hand into a damp foam mattress sticky with salt. A feeling that had begun in my stomach crept upwards, catching in my throat. What was I doing in this place for four months?

A month ago, on that warm spring day when Anne interviewed me for the job, it had seemed like a great adventure—

studying puffins on a remote island off the northwest tip of Vancouver Island. Confidently I assured her that I was strong, could work hard and was not worried about being isolated. When she called me the next day I was elated.

I took a deep breath. Pushing my rising panic down, I silently reviewed all the things that had to be done before nightfall.

Clouds descended from the summit as we scurried back and forth with gear. The wind tore sheets of rain from the sky and wrapped them around us. By the time all the boxes were under cover we were drenched.

Anne pulled the pieces of a new airtight stove out of a box, then sat on the grimy linoleum floor with a screwdriver in one hand and a page of small print and diagrams in the other. A francophone, she struggled over the English instructions, but she did not ask for my help.

As she concentrated, I found a hammer, stepped outside and climbed an old barrel onto the roof to pry off the wood covering the chimney hole. When we hauled the old stove out, the top crumbled into red powder. By the time we stood the new one in its place, darkness was pooling in the corners. Anne lit a candle on the windowsill, crumpled up the instruction sheet and stuffed it in the firebox, adding a few pieces of dry wood from a stack under the table. With the drafts wide open the little stove chugged like a locomotive and quickly became red hot. The steam from our wet clothes hanging above condensed on the black windows. Rain beat hard on the tin roof. We sat in our tiny circle of light, surrounded by a sea of darkness.

April 29

I pushed my way up through sleep heavy as water, toward light and the sound of surf, opened my eyes, and stared at a ceiling inches from my face. For a moment I didn't know where I was; then I recognized the faded plywood of the upper bunk. Outside the window, grey seeped from a watercolour sky into the bay.

Anne's bunk was empty. I fumbled for the warm ball of clothes in the toe of my sleeping bag and pulled them on. She was in the kitchen, digging a can of coffee out of the bottom of an unpacked box. As I watched her fill the coffee pot under the spout of a plastic water container, and set it on a two-burner propane stove, I remembered we had to find water today; we only had five gallons.

I reached for the loaf of bread we left out last night. The crust had been chewed off. The significance of the latched cupboard suddenly became clear.

As I put it back in the bag and fastened the twist tie, Anne picked up a crumpled piece of lined paper I recognized from our shopping trips.

"I think we need to be sure everything is here before we pack it away," she said. As she began checking items on the list, I secretly studied her pale, lightly freckled face. Still unfamiliar to me, it was difficult to read. Until now the only time we had spent together had been spent dashing around hardware stores, filling up grocery carts and packing box after box in her basement. We hadn't talked of anything personal. We had been too preoccupied with the thousand details of preparing for a long, complicated isolation, where nothing forgotten could be replaced.

I had returned home at the end of those days exhausted. The separation ahead frayed the edges of my relationship with Steven—it had been a relief to finally leave. Now I wasn't so sure. I tried to remember why I had wanted so badly for Anne to choose me among the students she interviewed for the job. I recalled a vision of myself on a cliff bathed in golden light, my hair blowing fetchingly in the wind, like a biologist in a National Geographic Special.

As I searched Anne's placid face for signs that she was sobered by the island's bleakness and our solitude I felt something slowly dawning on me: I was a hell of a long way from anywhere with a stranger for my sole companion. I could not change my mind and go home.

Anne straightened up and put her hands on her sturdy hips. I hoped she hadn't seen my anxiety. The coffee was perking. "Do you like coffee? I drink too much at home, but I won't be able to do that here," she laughed. We only had enough for one pot a day.

We sat sipping out of the mugs we found set upside down on the shelf above the propane stove and surveyed the chaos of half-unpacked boxes. Anne's mouth turned down slightly at the corners in concentration as she checked off items on a list of supplies: flour, pasta, milk powder, eggs, canned goods, spices… with no refrigeration fresh supplies would dwindle quickly. We had provisioned as if setting off to sea for four months.

All morning we buried onions, carrots and potatoes in buckets of sand. We smeared blocks of cheese with oil and wrapped them tightly in plastic to keep them from going moldy. We stacked shelves with cans of tomatoes, beans, peaches, bottles of oil, soya sauce, and lemon juice. We poured flour, sugar, and rice into plastic tubs.

In the afternoon we pulled on sweaters and rain gear, grabbed an empty water container and set off in search of the spring. As I stepped onto the beach, the wind dove down the back of my neck. I pulled my hood up and looked back at the island. Our trailer sat on a strip of flat land, wedged between the beach and steep slopes. I knew from maps that much of the island fell abruptly to the sea, but here on the south side the beach ran almost its whole length, about a mile. It seemed impossible that this small island was British Columbia's biggest seabird colony. Each spring birds that spent most of their lives at sea succumbed to the island's pull. More than a million seabirds nested here. A weathered sign nailed to a leaning post announced that the whole island was protected as an ecological reserve. It asked visitors not to go up into the breeding colonies.

My eyes followed the shore. At one end of the bay the island collapsed into a ruin of jagged reefs. At the other end was what the maps called "Puffin Rock." Tethered to the main island with narrow lengths of curved rock, it crouched like a sphinx, sleek flanks falling hundreds of feet into the sea, which was slowly eating it away. I could see a cut-out of the horizon through a hole the size of a train tunnel in its base.

We walked the tideline, trimmed with knee-high piles of seaweed, pungent with the smell of iodine. Crows picked through the day's tidal offerings, with one eye on the sky where an eagle slipped in silent circles. A cluster of vigilant seals, a few yards from shore, tracked us. When we approached, they flared their nostrils and slipped beneath the water, pulling it over their heads like a sweater.

Part One

A flock of gulls preening and shaking their feathers drew us to a small stream flowing from the base of the slope onto the beach. We set the open neck of the water container in the trickle and sat down with our elbows on our knees, watching the waves.

"Let's leave this here and go see Puffin Rock," Anne suggested a few minutes later, as she twisted the red cap onto the full container. She looked past me to the looming shape at the end of the beach.

I followed her gaze. The slopes looked impossibly steep. Against a tug of inner resistance, I picked up my pack and set off. I couldn't imagine how we were going to get to the top.

As we approached the base, the outline of a trail emerged. I took a deep breath and followed Anne, who was scrambling ahead, clinging to shrubs and clumps of dry, brittle grass.

"This is tufted hairgrass," she called down enthusiastically to me. "Puffins dig their nests into soil where it grows."

The trail wound up in steep switchbacks, cut into dark earth full of sharp stones. As I climbed, I was aware that a stumble would send me plummeting onto the rocks far below. I forced myself to think only of placing my feet carefully.

After twenty minutes of climbing we were about 200 feet above the beach. Anne disappeared over the lip above me. As I followed her, a fierce wind clawed at me. I pulled my wool hat from my coat pocket, jammed it on and scrambled over the top. Standing among the blowing grass, I slowly turned a full circle, taking in the view. To the east, the Scott Islands seemed like giant stepping stones cast into the sea to form a pathway back to Vancouver Island, lost now in layers of mist. To the north, the ridges of Triangle Island swept upward to its summit, crowned with the empty concrete tower of what was once the tallest, brightest lighthouse on the coast. To the south and west were grey plains of ocean stretching to a horizon heavy with the next dark bank of approaching clouds. Far below, in the crook of the beach's curving arm, was our tiny trailer.

The centre of the plateau on Puffin Rock, which from the helicopter appeared to be covered in a soft green pelt, revealed itself to be a dense tangle of chest-high, prickly salmonberry, just beginning to leaf out. We pulled our hands into our sleeves and

PUFFIN ROCK

the hole

pushed through narrow thorny trails, until we broke out into the open on the other side. The slopes were empty. The earth exuded a faint musky scent and I noticed for the first time that the ground was spongy with burrows. Some were marked with fresh digging and a few creamy streaks of droppings.

"From what I've heard, puffins nest on these slopes, but it's too early for them," Anne said, kneeling down, extending her arm into a narrow opening and feeling around in the dark. "It's so long I can't feel the end," she sighed, pulling her arm out and brushing off the damp soil. "These must be Cassin's auklet burrows. They lay their eggs in April."

Cassin's auklets are small grey and white seabirds about the size of a robin. More than half the world's population nest on Triangle Island.

I looked around at the empty meadows. "Where are they?"

Anne told me they were nocturnal, coming and going in the dark. I confessed it hadn't occurred to me that I wouldn't see the

Part One

trail up?

island's most numerous birds. "Don't worry, you'll get to see them," she said, explaining that she had agreed to collect food samples for the Canadian Wildlife Service when the birds began feeding their chicks. I wondered how on earth we'd do that, but she offered no further explanation.

We walked to the edge of the slope and I nestled into a grassy nook, out of the wind, pulling my knees to my chin. I would ask her later. For now I wanted to take in everything around me. Below me, the slopes became steeper and steeper until they gave way to walls of cliffs. I lifted my binoculars. A few pelagic cormorants clustered on narrow ledges, their dark oily feathers gleaming like taffeta. They turned nervously to look at us, arching their sinuous, womanly necks, and dropped off the rock face.

Anne scanned the land and sea carefully, looking for puffins. But they were nowhere to be seen. Except for the cormorants and gulls, the place was deserted.

We climbed back down the switchbacks and over the rocks at

the bottom just as the storm rolled in. The rain plastered my coat and pants against my back and legs, and I remembered deliberating over rain gear at an outdoor store the week before. When I mentioned to the sales clerk that I was going to Triangle Island, he raised his eyebrows. As he told me about the summer he worked on a fish boat in these waters, he carefully guided me away from the fashionable rain gear to a rack at the back of the store where rows of ugly, heavy green slickers hung above shelves of black rubber gumboots with thick orange soles.

At the door I shook water from my sleeves and grabbed the waistband of my rain pants to roll them down carefully, trying not to let my jeans get wet. I pulled off my coat and brought it inside to hang near the stove.

As I lit the fire, Anne carefully lifted a hard plastic case the size of a shoebox from a backpack on her bunk. She drew out a VHF radio and set it up just as she had been instructed, connecting it to a car battery and extending the short antenna. Then she turned it on and clicked the channel knob to two, where we should be able to contact Holberg on northern Vancouver Island. The operator would receive our signal, answer us and patch our call into the telephone system.

Anne adjusted the squelch button until the background static almost disappeared, then deliberately pressed down the call switch on the hand-held mike. Rrrring. "Hello, this is Holberg, over."

Her face relaxed. "This is Triangle Island, over."

She talked to her supervising professor in Vancouver, describing our trip, and assuring him that all was well. Then she called her family in Quebec.

"Allo, ici Anne."

A woman's voice burst through the static, in rapid-fire French. Anne smiled, her blue-grey eyes focussing beyond the window. I strained to pick up the few words I understood, "Oui, oui, je vais très bien, mais le temps est très mal."

A girl's voice broke in. Anne asked her something about her younger brother and they laughed.

When she hung up, I took the mike, still warm from her hand. I was longing to talk with Steven. Rrrring. "This is Holb—" The voice dissolved in a crackling blur. Each time I tried the same thing happened.

Part One

"Maybe it's the bad weather," Anne suggested as I crawled into my narrow sleeping bag, dejected.

I lay in the dark listening to the wind. Its fierce gusts shook our trailer. For a moment I stretched out motionless, feeling the tiredness in my muscles from climbing and carrying. Rolling over on my elbows, I lit a candle and reached for the bookshelf beside my bed. From between a tattered copy of *The Alexandria Quartet* and my sketch book I pulled a narrow red volume, an empty journal. I bent the stiff new spine open and scrawled: *here I am, just as I dreamed, on Triangle Island…*

May 2

"Damn!" I slipped, bruising my kneecap on a boulder. I adjusted my pack, sagging under the forty-pound car battery, and staggered on. Behind me, Anne carried the radio in its case. I cursed its inscrutable heart of tangled wire. Try as we might, we could not get it to work. Perhaps if we set it up at the base of Puffin Rock, we would get a better line of sight to Holberg.

After nestling it in the rock cleft and reconnecting it to the battery, I pressed the call button hopefully. The operator answered, a voice from the bottom of a well: "This is Holberg, you're breaking up, over." My hopes blew away in the wind. Though I shouted like a fishwife, she could not hear me. Discouraged, we covered the radio and battery with a plastic tarp, picked up our packs and walked back down the beach.

By the time we returned to the trailer the day's first raindrops were falling. We settled into an afternoon of reading. I picked a book about bird behaviour off the shelf and began reading: "About 13 percent of all the birds in the world are colonial nesters, but 93 percent of all marine birds nest in colonies. This is probably because they use the safe nesting sites provided by islands and cliffs…" I glanced over Anne's shoulder at the paper she was studying: *The Food, Feeding and Development of Young Tufted and Horned Puffins in Alaska.* The sound of rain on the roof, like a ticking clock, made the silence more profound.

"Anne?"

She looked up. I searched for a question.

"Did you always live in Quebec?"

"Yes, all my life," she answered, turning back to her work.

Suddenly I felt adrift, the loneliness about to close over my head—my only lifeline the sound of another voice.

"Did you have a happy childhood?" Anne looked at me with surprise, as if no one had ever asked her that question, as if she had never thought about it. She put down her reading.

"Yes, of course. My sisters and my brother and I do a lot together when I am home. I guess we are"—she searched for the English term—"a close family." She explained that she'd lived at home until last year. She came to Vancouver at twenty-one to begin her graduate work.

Anne picked up her paper again. Desperate to hang on to the thread of our conversation I said, "I moved around a lot as a kid."

She looked at me tentatively, as if she was not used to easy confidences. I felt a need to be known. She listened, nodding, while I carried on, relating how we'd moved constantly from town to town until I was ten, when my family had settled on Vancouver Island. At twenty-three, I had long since left home.

I told her how I had met Steven, when I was a park naturalist. He was working for what he called a "hoods in the woods" program, rehabilitating kids in trouble by getting them out of the city and leading them on a series of gruelling hikes and climbs. When I described our first dates, in the company of a dozen juvenile delinquents, Anne laughed.

"Do you have a boyfriend?" I asked tentatively.

"Yes, his name is Rob."

"Do you think you'll miss him?"

She looked thoughtful for a moment. "We haven't been going out for long. In the last weeks before I left, we hardly saw each other. I guess I was just too busy with everything…"

The rain ticked on. Anne bent her head over her reading. I opened *The Alexandria Quartet* to the first page: "The sea is high again today, with a thrilling flush of wind. In the midst of winter you can feel the inventions of spring."

May 3

Life became reduced to its simplest elements—work, sleep, shelter, food—punctuated by small rituals and routines: the alarm at six, the one rationed cup of morning coffee, the one channel from Prince Rupert on the transistor. We heard about town meetings, fishing openings, boating disasters and company picnics in the remote coastal city north of us.

After breakfast we made a lunch to stuff in our day packs along with binoculars, spotting scopes, field notebooks and rain gear, and set off to explore parts of the island where nesting puffins had been seen in other years. But it was impossible to choose study plots until the birds landed. They usually arrived in the first half of May. Scrambling over the island, I longed to see the empty slopes peppered with puffins.

At lunch one day we sat on the ridgetop in the wind, unwrapping our sandwiches. The sea was empty, except for a small grey smudge on the horizon, the plume of a far-off freighter, perhaps headed for the Orient.

"My grandfather was lost crossing the Pacific once," I said, handing Anne the Thermos of tea. I told her how the ship's cargo, Douglas fir from the old-growth forests of coastal British Columbia, shifted, flooding the engine room. The freighter was found a few days later, drifting without power, and all were rescued—except my grandfather and ten other men. They had volunteered to try to make it to land in a lifeboat. For fifteen days, my distraught grandmother, pregnant with my father, heard nothing. She had given him up for dead by the time the call came. The whaleboat was picked up a day's travel from San Francisco's Golden Gate Bridge. The crew had rowed 950 miles, surviving the longest stretch on record in an open boat in the north Pacific.

"I'd never seen the Pacific until I came to Vancouver," Anne admitted.

I had spent most of my life living on its rim, yet looking out over its reaches, I realized that what I knew was what I might know of the sky through a chimney hole.

Anne screwed the top back on the Thermos and began packing up the empty lunch things. I watched the freighter's plume slip over the curved lens of the sea and disappear, then turned back to the windblown island.

In the trailer, I dumped a damp pile out of my pack onto the table—the first lady fern shoots, collected on the way home. They were coiled tight as springs and covered in rust-coloured fuzz. I turned to our bookshelves, and ran my finger lightly over their spines: birds, intertidal life, fish, plants, geology. I pulled out a slender paperback, *Food Plants of Coastal Peoples*, by Nancy Turner.

West Coast tribes steamed ferns in pits then dipped them in seal oil and ate them with dried salmon eggs. I contemplated the slightly bitter taste of the steamed ferns. They didn't seem any worse than the meat we had left—a hard, dry length of sausage, almost black on the outside. The crows and gulls had devoured the pork chops we left on the beach. They had gone bad before we could eat them.

After dinner I fought the urge to curl up by the stove, resolved to have a bath. I carried a pot of hot water outside, quickly stripped down and poured a couple of cups over myself. Shivering in the wind, I soaped up, doused myself with two more cups of rinse water, towelled off frantically, and pulled clothes over my damp skin. Leaning over the pot, I wet my hair, and worked in shampoo. Using the carefully conserved water to rinse it out, I rubbed my hair dry and hurried back inside to the warmth.

Anne handed me the scissors. "Would you cut off my hair please?"

"You mean trim it?"

"No, leave it this long." She held up her fingers two inches apart.

Reluctantly I took the scissors. "You're sure you won't mind how you look when I'm done?"

"No. I just don't want to have to worry about washing and brushing it."

As I snipped away at Anne's shoulder length hair, a drift of fine blond curls gathered on the floor. When I finished she looked like a young novitiate. I wondered whether I should ask her to do the same, and ran my hands through my long brown hair a moment, wrestling with my vanity. As Anne picked up a mirror to examine herself, I caught my own reflection: an oval face with ruddy cheeks. Hazel eyes, under dark eyebrows, looked back at me, almost surprised—I hadn't glanced in a mirror for days.

I turned away, scooped up the feathery pile of Anne's hair, stepped outside and let it fly into the darkness. Perhaps a songbird would line a nest with it.

May 5

Anne unfolded the topo map. Getting to the lighthouse, by any approach, would be a hard scramble.

"I think it's possible to get there by heading straight up here." She gazed up at the steep pitch behind the trailer.

We shouldered our packs, took deep breaths and started climbing. Within an hour we reached the backbone of the island and turned to follow its upward sweep. Open meadows soon ran into a wall of wind-tangled salmonberry and crabapple. There was no trail; our only choice was to push our way through. Spiny twigs tore at my clothes and hair. A sea of thorns closed over my head.

I stopped and listened for the sound of cracking branches. "Anne! Where are you?"

"Over here." A muffled voice called from somewhere ahead. Panicky, I held my arms out in front of me, and looked up through the lattice of leaves, trying to orient myself with the sun.

Eventually, hot and dishevelled, scratched and bleeding, we broke into a clearing. A high-pitched, angry scream startled us— a peregrine falcon disappeared in a dark streak behind a grey tower silhouetted against high cloud.

The island fell away in dizzying contours, the sea and sky spinning out around us. I tried to imagine what it must have been like to live on this bare and solitary summit. Did lightkeepers haul water up or collect rainwater? What kind of meals could they make on cold fires, with stale supplies? How did they fill the long winter nights? Where did they go when they wanted to escape the wide stare of sky?

We climbed onto the tall cement foundations of scattered outbuildings. The walls of houses where the lightkeepers' families and radio operators lived had long fallen. In fireplaces, which they couldn't keep alight in the howling winds, yellow flames of tufted hairgrass bristled. We walked the narrow ledges, placing each foot carefully in front of the other, leaping gingerly over gaps that were once doorways. If we slipped, the dense labyrinth of salal bushes below would swallow us.

Nearby was a crumbling metal cylinder the size of a large water heater—an old steam donkey engine, falling in upon itself in flakes, consumed by the slow fire of rust. Once it had run a winch that hauled supplies up a ton and a half of steel rail tracks from the beach. I looked for the tracks and found them, snaking into the undergrowth. They emerged a few hundred yards farther. A wave of vertigo engulfed me as I traced the scar on the north flank of the island where they dropped, steep as a roller coaster, to the shore far below.

As we approached the lighthouse I tried to make out the faded names of ships. On fine days in other summers, crews made it up here to spray-paint in red and black: *Lorna B., Sea Warrior, Miss Mel…*

The tower was dark and damp, hollow as a flute played by the wind. Dry gusts whistled into high windows. The ascending staircase and the famous light—with outer prisms nine feet in circumference, which turned on a tub filled with 900 pounds of mercury—were gone. But the lighthouse still had a dignified air of grandeur. Its supporting buttresses swept up in graceful curves; the lintel of the door still bore, under felted moss and garlands of ferns, its classical ornamentation and "AD 1910" in roman script.

The story, ending in slow decay on the windy summit of Triangle Island, began in 1909 as one of the most ambitious projects in the history of navigation on this coast. In *Keepers of the Light* Donald Graham describes how the vision of this lighthouse had consumed W.P. Anderson, the Marine Department's chief engineer. The first landfall for ships using the trans-Pacific Great Circle route would be crowned with a one-million-candlepower light.

From the beginning, Triangle was ominous. A skeleton with lifebelt, tattered rags of clothes and sea boots greeted the lighthouse work crew when they explored one of the island's sea caves. The waters around Triangle sweep from the straits of the Queen Charlotte Islands to the north and Vancouver Island to the

remains of the old lighthouse

east, swirling together to create huge tide rips and wicked currents. Combined with the high winds and storms for which this area is famous, these seas could transform from flat calm to furious boil within a few hours. The corpse could have been one of many men lost near the island.

On the summit, 600 feet above the sea, workers battled fierce winds to hammer up forms for the forty-six-foot tower, mix and pour cement, and blast for water cisterns. They had to frame a house as well as a wireless shack, as Triangle Island was to be a crucial telegraph station, relaying messages between Prince Rupert and the capital, Victoria.

As we stood in the tower's musty darkness, I dug my toe into the damp earth, dislodging a raven feather and a cigarette butt. It was hard to imagine this place ringing with the voices of children. Mary Davies, one of the first lightkeeper's daughters, described that time:

> As children we took life on Triangle Island in stride, though my mother was driven to distraction at times by the difficulties of the place...We were a lighthouse family, and when the time came to move to Triangle the prospect of living on a bleak island didn't worry us at all. But I must admit we found that Triangle was unique in many ways...Hurricane winds for days on end, gales and fog for weeks at a time—these things can be hard to bear, even with the resiliency of childhood, when there's only very restricted freedom of movement.

In 1912 the family endured a storm in which the anemometer clocked the wind at 120 miles per hour before the instrument was torn from its fastenings and hurled over the cliff. The wireless mast shattered and flew through the air. Six brick and iron chimneys were sheared off, and a shed next to the lighthouse left its moorings, rolled end over end and tumbled into the sea. The wind shook the wireless operators' house until it split in two forcing them to crawl between buildings on their stomachs to join the children and their mother crouched together, their house rocking back and forth, the glass in the windows bulging inwards.

"I'm glad we live on the beach," I said, and Anne nodded. From here our shelter, huddled in the shadow of this summit, looked cozy; our simple fare seemed extravagant when I thought of many months without fresh food. Mr. Davies had once ordered a large shipment of fresh fruit and vegetables. It finally arrived, somehow buried under tons of coal in the ship's hold; only two apples and half a banana survived. Mrs. Davies had tried many times to grow a garden. Seeds would sprout bravely but soon withered in the poor soil and incessant wind. Supplies often dwindled perilously low when foul weather kept ships away from Triangle's tricky shores.

Sometimes boats had to run the risk. One February night a wireless message implored Victoria to send help immediately for Mrs. Davies. Weak from hemorrhage, she was lashed to a mattress, lowered down the steep rail tracks, rowed by crewmen through rough water to a lighthouse tender standing offshore, and hoisted onto its rolling decks.

The difficulty of landing on the island created other hardships. Radio operators balked at being sent to Triangle Island. Though they were supposed to serve six months, most operators spent nine months or more before leaving, their posts extended while boats waited for settled weather. Some claimed that they were "shanghaied" to the station; they were told they were going there on relief for a week, so ended up with only a suitcase full of clothes to last them several months. After less than three years on the island Mr. Davies begged for a transfer, writing, "Triangle is very hard on our nerves and a great strain on our constitutions."

By this time it must have been obvious to the Marine Department that Triangle's lighthouse was not only difficult to staff but not always helpful to mariners. Still, it would take a tragedy to topple it from its high perch.

A few years and two lightkeepers later, the government steamer *Galiano* called at the island to drop off supplies and to pick up two passengers: Sidney Elliott, one of the operators, and a Miss Brunton, teacher to the lightkeeper's children and housekeeper for the wireless men for a year. Accompanying them to the beach was operator Jack Neary, who welcomed the chance to talk to his brother Michael, radio operator on the ship. Sid Elliot learned from the crew that his shift was to be continued. As he climbed back up to the wireless station, his bitter disappointment must have grown with each of the thousand steps. As the weather began to build, the crew rushed to finish unloading and to deliver

Miss Brunton to the *Galiano*, standing well offshore. The lucky lady aboard, the ship cast off, her stern light disappearing as she plied north through rough seas to her next stop in the Queen Charlotte Islands.

At 3:30 a.m. Triangle received a message from Michael Neary. Desperately, he signalled his brother: HOLD FULL OF WATER. SEND HELP. Though the operators tried to reach them all night, the ship never responded; it went down with all twenty-nine men and Miss Brunton.

The loss of the *Galiano* made it difficult to ignore the problem of Triangle Island. Although it was the tallest, brightest light on the coast, it was not reliable. In his effort to build the ultimate lighthouse, W.P. Anderson had broken one of the primary rules of lighthouse design—never build higher than 150 feet. Towering almost 700 feet above the sea, the light was not visible when it was needed most—in fog. A decade after the Herculean effort of establishing it, the Department of Marine and Fisheries finally decided to extinguish Triangle's light. The wireless station persisted for two more years, then it, too, closed down. Triangle Island was left to the birds.

May 8

The wind, which had been blowing all morning in a fitful, cranky way from the southeast, built steadily. Absorbed in my work, checking burrows for any sign of birds, I didn't see the line spreading like an eclipse over the sea. When I finally glanced up, the glaucous-winged gulls, still caught in sunlight, were brilliant white, hovering stationary against the black sky.

I went to look for Anne, working on the next plot. She was nowhere to be seen. Unconcerned, I crossed to the windward side of Puffin Rock, where 40-knot gusts blew the birds out of the sky—air and land were empty. Dark clouds fastened themselves to the horizon and the sunlight faded. I stuffed my hair into my hood, yanked on the strings to gather it tightly around my face, and leaned into wind serrated now with rain. Didn't gentle breezes ever blow here? I scanned the grass for Anne's blue jacket. The bare slopes and dark cliffs were gothic, ominous. I wished I

was somewhere lovely, having tea among delphiniums and foxgloves, wearing a white dress and a straw hat that didn't have to be tied on firmly.

Anne was not there. I tried to calm a muffled beating, like captive wings, inside my ribcage, and decide on a plan of action. I would visit each slope, one by one. If I didn't find her I would walk to the top of the trail, in case she was waiting for me there.

I finally found her on her hands and knees near a little wooden A-frame blind. She had looped lengths of rope over and around it, and was pushing stakes into the ground nearby.

"Help me tie these down!" she shouted, the wind immediately swallowing her words.

We didn't want to lose this blind. We had built it the day before, after wrestling the heavy plywood up the steep trail by rope. The storm was threatening to pick it up and hurl it onto the rocks below. We caught ends of the rope, which were lashing back and forth, and fastened them as well as we could to the stakes, then scrambled off the exposed slope quickly, looking back at the blind, rocking precariously. By now the wind was blowing fifty knots. The sea was caught in a white gale, veiled in spray and great patches of foam blowing in dense streaks downwind.

According to the *Mariner's Weather Log*, which had been left in the trailer, the tempest spiralling over Triangle Island was unusual for that time of year. In May and June storms normally subside and the Pacific finally begins to live up to its gentle name. By this time the Pacific High, an area of high pressure, which winters at sea, off the coast of California, has expanded northwards. By July it would encompass almost the entire northeast Pacific, bringing fair weather and northwest winds; the water would begin to absorb heat. By August the power of the sun to continue heating the water would fail, but water has a long memory and even then the ocean would be pregnant with winter storms. Slowly it would begin to release its warmth. Air, forgetting its past more readily, disperses the heat in restless movement, fuelling fall storms.

By November, long after Anne and I would have left the island, the low pressure cell over the Bering Sea known as the Aleutian Low would edge its huge grey body into the Gulf of Alaska, stirring the ocean, turning over the layers, harvesting summer heat. By January the low is massive, wedged over the farthest Aleutians, with fierce counter-clockwise winds howling around its dark centre. Gale after gale would spin off it, lashing the deserted island.

The simple language and unadorned facts of the *Weather Log* painted a portrait of the north Pacific's relentless weather. Crews of tankers, freighters and deep-sea fishing boats commonly reported sixty-knot winds, with thirty-five-foot waves breaking over the decks.

More storm systems followed the gale that blew us down Puffin Rock. We lived in a world without colour, a world pressed flat beneath the sky's white palm. If the clouds broke during the day, they soon knit themselves back together. If the night sky cleared, it was lightless, the new moon hanging like an unlit torch.

Dusk descended without shadow, the light draining slowly. I took our small Coleman lantern from its nail by the window, wishing I had a way to call the fair wind—as the people of this coast once had—with charms of crabs, starfish, ferns or snails hung in groups of four over the fire. I set the lantern on the counter, pumped it half a dozen times and turned the knob until the propane hissed inside the glass panes. Digging the matches out of my pocket, I struck one and held it to the small opening, waiting until the frail cloth mantle suspended within caught the flame, trembled and began to roar gently.

I hung the lantern on its nail above the window and picked up *Pilgrim at Tinker Creek* from the counter where I had left it the night before. "There are seven or eight categories of phenomena in the world that are worth talking about, and one of them is weather," I read.

I was tired of weather. There was no escape from it here. The wind flew down the chimney with a low moan. Anne, sitting at one end of the counter, making notes, looked up.

"It sounds like wolves are at the door," she laughed.

"At least that's not something we have to worry about here."

"I love wolves," Anne said.

I looked at her, surprised.

"I spent some time helping a friend of mine who was studying them, in northern Quebec. We would go out in the snow at night and listen to them calling." She sighed, and looked off into the dark. "I would've been happy to study wolves."

It had never occurred to me to study a large mammal like wolves. I thought of the women biologists I had met. They were microbiologists, botanists or ecologists. There were a few zoologists and ornithologists, but women studying raptors like eagles or peregrines were rare and large mammals even rarer.

A semester away from finishing my biology degree, I had no idea what I would do afterward. I always imagined I would work on living things. This summer I would find out if I was cut out for field work.

"Why did you decide to study seabirds?" I asked, remembering that we had talked during our first interview only about why *I* wanted to come to Triangle Island.

She leaned her chin on her hand. "I got a job as a naturalist in the Gaspé one summer. I used to watch the gannet colonies. By the end of the summer I knew I wanted to study seabirds…and then when I got the scholarship, I could choose where I wanted to go. Triangle Island seemed like an amazing place with lots of work still to be done."

She shrugged modestly when I asked her about the award, which I recognized as one given to just a few graduates each year. As she bent her head once more over her papers, I pulled myself close to the light to read my book, turning the damp pages.

I looked up at the window. My pale face gazed back at me, below the lantern's yellow light. Outside the wind continued to howl. Loneliness settled on me, a small weight I could not shed.

May 10

We nestled ourselves among grass hummocks, and reached into our packs for sandwiches. Suddenly, the curtain of clouds pulled back. Triangle's bitter brown slopes turned golden. The ocean was sequined with silver light.

Anne watched the bay intently through her binoculars. "Look down there." She pointed to the water far below. A small group of compact black birds floated, silhouetted against the sunlit water. I caught a flash of orange beak.

"Puffins!"

By the time we returned home, the clouds had drawn themselves closed again. The birds bobbed in the dark troughs of the bay. I threw down my pack, reached up to the shelf above the stove for a bottle of rum, and poured two inches into scratched plastic glasses, along with a shot of Tang.

"Oh," Anne said, "I almost forgot."

She rifled through her pack among sweatshirts and wool socks, and pulled out fistfuls of pale, diaphanous cloth.

"We should dress up, don't you think?" She held out two thrift store skirts.

Surprised, I took a lilac-coloured chiffon. Anne's face, usually so composed and serious, lit up. I realized that she had been preparing for this moment for a long time. The arrival of the birds was the beginning of her own research, and of her career as a biologist. I handed her a glass and she curtsied clumsily in her gumboots.

We sat on the rickety plank bench in front of the trailer, with our skirts blowing around our legs, lifted our glasses and toasted the puffins.

On the water, they floated in their own finery—black coats, jewel-like bills, and golden facial tassels. Compact, sleek and natty, they looked like they shared a tailor with penguins.

By now I had learned that puffins belong to a different family of birds, the alcids. This family, at home in northern waters around the globe, includes the horned puffin and the Atlantic puffin, as well as murres, murrelets, guillemots, dovekies, razorbills and auklets. In fact, the name penguin was originally the Gaelic name for the great auk, the largest member of the alcid family. Like penguins, the great auk was flightless. Hunted relentlessly by sailors, the last reported sighting of a great auk was off Newfoundland in 1852. Only the name penguin lives on, given to the similar but unrelated birds of the southern hemisphere.

Like penguins, alcids wear a dusky cloak of camouflage on the dark sea. Many have white breasts and bellies, to blend into the bright light flooding the ocean surface when viewed from below, helping them to surprise prey and escape predators. Often, like the puffins, they sport facial plumes, tufts or bright beaks.

For larger alcids, like puffins, the resemblance to penguins extends beyond similar plumage. In the cold waters of high latitudes these unrelated groups have evolved similar fat bodies with short, stubby wings adapted for underwater pursuit of fish. Penguins, in fact, became such skillful underwater predators that they lost their ability to fly. Puffins can fly, but, because of their small wings, have difficulty getting airborne. For this reason, they nest on slopes from which they can "fall" when they take off, getting immediate lift. The meadows of Triangle are ideal puffin nesting grounds. They are steep, with soft soil that can be easily excavated for burrows. The island's remoteness has kept it free of predators like cats, rats, and raccoons, which can decimate ground-nesting birds. Triangle Island, such an inhospitable home to humans, is a rare safe haven for seabirds.

May 14

More puffins arrived, blackening the waters around the island. We watched them from shore. At first they spent most of their time drifting idly, or sleeping with their heads tucked under their wings, exhausted by their long journey. Gradually the birds were drawn to land. We watched their first flights over the colonies. A few birds circled, all flying in the same direction. Each day they were joined by more, until the flock swelled into a dark halo of thousands of birds. The solitary winter habits of the puffins were suspended. On Triangle Island they became social creatures.

I sat in the grass, mesmerized by the endless wheels. Far below I heard the thrum of the surf, above me the thin, high sound of puffins' wings tearing the air. In the circling flocks, which protect the arriving and departing puffins from avian predators like eagles and peregrines, the birds seemed to be battling the impulse to touch down, for the first time in many months, on land. They tilted their heads this way and that, scanning the terrain below them. Finally, one by one, they banked into the wind, spread their webbed feet and dropped, in what looked like narrowly averted crash landings.

If we sat quietly they landed within a yard or two of us. Nesting for centuries on islands free of predators, puffins have little innate fear, making them easy to hunt. For many people living near seabird colonies in the North Sea, puffins were an

a pair of tufted puffins lounging among hummocks of grass in front of their burrow.

important part of the diet. One diner described the meat as "excellent…the breast is the meatiest portion, and this part and the thighs of two puffins will provide a man with enough meat for a meal." In the Faeroes, as many as half a million birds a year were taken around the turn of the century by fowlers armed with dogs and long-handled nets. They were brought home, where children removed heads, wings and feet. Women plucked 200 to 300 puffins, often with their teeth (inadvertently swallowing a pound of feathers a year). The Inuit of Greenland ate puffins raw or skinned them and stuffed them in bags of sealskin with the blubber still attached. They were said to be especially delicious after a few months of aging in a cool place, when the birds had melted into the seal fat. The puffins of Triangle Island may have been eaten by the coastal people. Even at the turn of the century, long after the Scott Islands were inhabited, Triangle was still a traditional site for harvesting seabird eggs. Puffins, along with other seabirds, only became protected by international treaty in the 1970s.

The puffins landing in the grass near me were almost close enough to touch. I could see clearly the details of the beak, brilliant orange at the tip, shading into green at the base. A white facemask extends back from the beak, terminating in silky facial tufts. At rest, the tufts lie over the neck like two golden kiss curls; in a wind they blow lightly about the bird's head; in flight they stream straight back. The green eye with its crisp black pupil is outlined in crimson. The breast and back are coal black. The sturdy, webbed feet are, like the beak, bright orange. Their stocky bodies are inflated at the chest by heavy muscles, which drive the strong stubby wings in underwater flight. The legs are placed "far-aft," making them awkward on land. With their waddling gait, short wings tucked behind their backs, oversized beaks and hoary tufts, they are black-robed judges wearing clown noses.

On these first visits they were anxious on land. They looked as if they couldn't imagine what had come over them, dropped off the slopes, wheeled again and returned to the safety of the sea.

On the waters below, birds swam in pairs, nuzzling each other's bills and tossing their heads. One bird swimming in pursuit of another caught my eye. I followed its determined zigzag through my binoculars. After a few half-hearted dives, the leading bird allowed her pursuer to overtake her and flutter onto her back.

His weight pushed her stern down into the water, tilting her breast up. He held his body upright, twisted his tail down and pressed it onto her underside, flapping his wings ecstatically. Just when it looked as if she would sink under his exertions, she swam out from under him and shook her ruffled feathers. It is one of the mysteries of puffin courting that copulation appears to occur only on the water and not in the privacy of burrows.

I wondered if this couple were veterans of many summers on Triangle Island. Puffins, which can live more than twenty years, probably keep their mates. Little is known about their lives at sea, but it is hard to imagine that pairs could remain together through the storms that rage over their wintering grounds in the north Pacific. The slight differences between individuals, which may be important for mate recognition, are lost in the winter: the birds drop their colourful beak plates and shed their facial plumes; their white masks turn dusky, and they become nondescript.

Each spring, the intelligence peculiar to birds—an appreciation of sun, wind and stars, an acute sense of time, perhaps a sensitivity to the tug of the magnetic pole—guides them back to the breeding grounds. It is likely that the pairs find each other again here, and rendezvous at old nest sites.

Day by day the puffins spent more time on land, as if waking from a pelagic dream. They began the work of nesting: tentatively inspecting burrows, then excavating with feet and beaks, sending earth flying.

Some pairs were at old nest sites. Some had claimed new ones. Others were house hunting. Residents had to protect their burrows; if an intruder approached, the owner usually puffed itself up, opening beak and wings slightly. For puffins, almost silent birds with simple plumage, the beak is a flag with which they signal each other. Turning the bill away is an appeasing gesture; holding the head forward and slightly down and raising the neck feathers, a threat display. If a challenger persists, birds can end up in battle, beaks locked, sometimes tumbling down the slope until they free themselves, usually unhurt.

As the puffins began the breeding season in earnest, we began our work identifying the nesting areas for study over the summer. Research in Newfoundland suggested that gull populations, growing fat on landfills and fish factories, were affecting puffin

Part One

colonies. Atlantic puffins feeding their young were being harassed by hungry gulls into dropping their fish. Biologists coined the term "kleptoparasitism" to describe the gulls' thieving habits. Anne was interested in whether gulls were kleptoparasitizing puffins on Triangle Island and whether steep nesting sites, where puffins could get into their burrows quickly, were an advantage. Over the summer we would carefully observe gulls and puffins, and choose sites where we could measure burrows, weigh eggs, and track the growth of chicks.

First we had to survey as many areas as we could. We became connoisseurs of droppings, feathers, and burrow architecture. Tufted puffin droppings are whitish or yellowish; their burrows usually take one or two turns before settling into a large nest cup cradling a single egg. On our hands and knees we moved over the guano-stained slopes, rolling on one shoulder and sticking our arms into any openings we could find. Grass tips speared our ears and eyes. Anxious gulls nesting nearby flew over us, screaming. Shooters of warm, foul smelling gull shit soaked into my scalp, trickling down my neck. "Merde!" I cursed, with one of the few French words I remembered from my childhood in northern

Part One

Ontario. Anne grimaced appreciatively. I ran my sleeve over my hair, pulled up my anorak hood and carried on.

When is a slope too steep, I wondered. This one looked like good nesting terrain—birds lounged in pairs in grass riddled with burrows—but it was more precipitous than any we had explored so far. Below it, cliffs hung in dark sheets.

I was growing used to the cliffs and had lost the vertigo I first felt working high above the sea. But, until now, we had surveyed slopes well back from drop-offs. I was nagged by the fear that, if one of us were injured, we had no way of calling for help. Our radio was still not working.

"Anne," I said, trying not to show my trepidation. "Do you think we should have protection on this one?"

Unruffled, she nodded. We walked to an old blind nearby, which collapsed years ago into a pyramid of grey, weathered planks covered in powdery green lichens. From under it we pulled an old climbing rope we found in the shed and carried up a few days ago. Beside it was a pile of five-foot lengths of rusted rebar, left by previous researchers.

Leaning into the wind, we returned to the top of the slope, and hunted for a heavy rock to pound the rebar into the soil. We cut the climbing rope in half, each of us taking about a hundred feet. I grabbed my stake and gave it a shake. It didn't come out, but it rocked gently back and forth. I wasn't sure it would hold my weight. On the other side of the slope Anne was patiently tying one end of her rope around her stake. I did the same, then began to tie the other end around my waist, wishing I had asked Steven to take me on more of his frequent climbing expeditions. I had no idea how to secure myself to a rope. Eventually I tied a snarl of knots which held when I pulled hard on them.

The puffins got up grumpily and flew off as I descended gingerly and began moving on my hands and knees, examining each burrow for the tell-tale signs of puffin housekeeping, making a mental note of the number I counted. Gradually I forgot that I was on an exposed slope—it wasn't until I got to the end of my rope and stood up that I realized I was a stride away from the cliff edge. For a moment I stared at the surf, hundreds of feet below. Swells slammed into black rocks, breaking into walls of spray that the wind plastered against the cliffs. As each wave sucked back, swimming-pool-sized green wells opened up around the reefs. I could hear the hiss of water pouring into them. With the next roller the wells filled and once again the air was shattered with spray. What would happen to a body falling into the teeth of those rocks? The ground swayed below me. I pulled my gaze away and forced myself to look at my feet. Crouching, I gave my rope a tug for reassurance, crawled back up and untied myself.

As we walked back Anne wondered aloud which research plots looked good, then pondered whether the timing of nest building was normal—she would look up the exact dates of previous years when she got back to the trailer. Concentrating on footholds and forced into single file by the narrow path, we fell silent.

Walking the long beach back and forth from Puffin Rock each day had become a meditation. At first fatigue numbed my mind. But over the last few weeks my body had become strong. My jeans hung loose on my hips and the muscles in my arms and legs had hardened. Now I walked easily, hardly winded. My mind, unaccustomed to such idleness, turned first to home. I wondered what Steven or my friends in the city were doing. They probably had no idea how much I longed for the most mundane things: a cold beer, a long hot bath, a movie. Eventually though, memories began to flood my thoughts, as if they had been dammed by a wall that was beginning to crumble under the weight of solitude. I remembered vividly the blue eyes and round face fringed with black hair, of Cleo, my bosom friend when I was five; I recalled jumping off a moving rail car and twisting my ankle when I was ten; I roamed the neighbourhoods I grew up in and walked through the rooms of each house; I examined the youthful faces of my mother and father before their hair turned grey. There seemed to be no end to what I had forgotten.

May 16

We had been on the island for only three weeks. Already all my clothes were filthy and my socks had holes in them. I had ripped the knee of one of my two pairs of pants when Anne and I tried to climb to the high ridges on the west of the island. According

Part One

to our map we could take a nifty shortcut over the top of the island and back down to our trailer. What the map didn't show was armpit-high crabapple, wind-gnarled into spiny, arthritic thickets that finally turned us back.

Back at the cabin I took stock. We had almost finished the coffee and become bored with our tapes. I had only the few folk and classical tapes I had thrown into my bags just as I was running out the door at home. Anne had brought music from Quebec, as well as some blues and rock. But her favourite tape she'd picked up from her new culture—we had listened to the *Rocky Horror Picture Show* so many times we knew the songs by heart.

I nursed my scratches, drank my small allotment of grog, and crawled into bed. Then I drifted off to sleep imagining a boat steaming into the bay, its hold full not of fish, but the items I had just listed wistfully in my journal:

new tapes
six pairs of wool socks
a month's supply of underwear
baby powder
a hot water bottle
a pillow with a flannel cover
a book of poetry
coffee
rum

May 18

"I wish I could find out what my friends back home think." Anne turned up the transistor.

I slumped at the table, still not fully awake. The early morning news was full of the Quebec referendum, which would be in less than a week. Would the province vote to separate from Canada?

I had to admit I was a little fuzzy on the issues. I had never been to Quebec, and didn't know much about its history or politics.

"What do you think will happen?" I asked.

"I don't know. It's all a little crazy, but still I feel like I'm missing all the excitement." Anne's family were pragmatic professionals, neither rural Quebecois, nor the idealistic intellectuals and artists of the separatist movement. It was a turbulent time in Quebec and I could see how carefully she listened for news, how much the unrest at home was on her mind.

Every morning before we climbed the trail we stopped to visit

spring rendezvous on the nesting slopes

Part One

our radio, sulking under its tarp at the base of the trail, to see if it had changed its mind. But it refused to work. All we knew of the world was what we heard on this transistor.

We were just finishing breakfast when Prince Rupert radio was interrupted by an emergency newscast. Mount St. Helens, in

southern Washington State, was erupting. A force equal to 27,000 atomic bombs had blown the top of the mountain off. Lava seared down the peak, melting hot scars in the spring snow pack, heading for forests. Frantic residents of nearby cities choked under a descending cloud of ash. Even people hundreds of miles away on Vancouver Island had felt the blast.

We had noticed nothing. We set down our bowls and spoons, walked outside, and stared at the hazy horizon.

Later, as we climbed to Puffin Rock, I turned and looked east, towards civilization, where people were dancing, scribbling memos, crying, picking up the week's groceries, singing, studying Italian, burying their dead, paying electricity bills. Trying to comprehend the multifarious present, the world humming in those far cities, was impossible. Easier to decipher the past.

Vancouver Island was a pale blue shadow crowned with pewter cloud. Below its towering conifer forests were its layers and scars. The small continent of Wrangellia, forged by eruptions at an oceanic "hot spot" like the Hawaiian Islands, had been dragged from near the equator by the Pacific plate. Moving at about the speed that fingernails grow, it probably arrived here at about the same time that the earth's first primitive birds were appearing, 160 million years ago. Parts of it broke away and moved north. Volcanoes continued to build what was left. Rain and ice eroded it.

I traced Triangle Island's profile against the sky. Its timeless quality was an illusion. Even here, the land we lived on slowly altered. Only 10,000 years ago, glaciers a mile thick stretched icy hands from the continent into these waters. Their prints remained on the sea floor as deep canyons and the discarded rubble of moraines.

At the top of the steep trail I looked towards the open sea. To the north, plates grinding past each other at the immense Queen Charlotte fault shuddered regularly with underwater earthquakes. Just past the horizon the continental shelf dropped into dark abyss. Beyond was a drowned landscape, restlessly making and remaking itself. A deep trench veering south to California patiently swallows old-crust ocean plate and thrusts it below the continent, where friction and heat sometimes blows the tops off inland volcanoes like pressure cooker valves.

Part One

West of the coastal trench, over sixty miles offshore, a line of submerged volcanic peaks rise more than 10,000 feet, their underwater eruptions creating new ocean floor. Some of these mountains almost break the surface, their summits circled by schools of fish turning like flocks of birds under a mirrored sky.

I tried to imagine the ocean basin, flooded countries of vertiginous peaks and valleys untouched by wind and rain. And the world beyond, more mysterious than the moon, a trench so deep that Mount Everest could fit into it with more than half a mile to spare.

I looked at the birds wheeling above me, spilling from the sky. Eventually, time would bury this land too. What seemed like an ageless match between creature and place was only a shared geological instant. Once this solitary edifice of dark stone was something else. I picked up a dusty shard of rock and turned it over in my hand. No one had studied these rocks, but geologists suspected that they contained fossils of microscopic marine creatures. Long before the earth dreamed of puffins, the dead bodies of these single-celled organisms, encased in shells of glassy-like silicon, drifted like a continuous snowfall onto an ancient ocean bottom. Eons later, when the Pacific plate to the west rammed itself under the continent, this floor sediment was peeled back and lifted. Triangle Island is believed to be a surviving fragment—a defiant thrust of land that had weathered ice ages, erosion, and the rise and fall of ocean levels. Like the tide of birds flooding here each spring, the last island belongs to the sea.

May 27

Anne stood at the window counter meticulously cutting up carrots and celery. Tonight she was making "Lentils, Monastery Style," a soup from *Diet for a Small Planet*, one of the few cookbooks we'd brought.

Beyond her was the scene so familiar to me now—steady pulse of waves, parentheses of land around the wide bay, empty sky.

"*Let's do the time warp again!*" the tape in the deck screamed. I groaned and dropped my head into my arms on the table.

"Anne, let's listen to something more mellow," I said, stretching over the counter to rummage among our music tapes.

"Try the one with the red label," she said as she poured lentils into a pot. It was one we somehow hadn't played yet.

"*Aujourd'hui je dis bonjour à la vie…*" A male voice, flute and guitar.

"What group is this?" I asked, leaning back against the wall and peeling off my damp socks.

"Harmonium. You don't know them?" She was surprised when I confessed I didn't.

"In Quebec they're famous, almost like the Beatles."

Anne and I could have grown up in different countries, speaking different languages, listening to different music, reading different books. For now, our nation was still the same—Quebec had rejected separation. She gazed out the window thoughtfully for a moment. "I think I'll make sugar pie."

I looked at her quizzically.

"It was my favourite dessert when I was a kid." She scanned the shelves. "You should have butter to mix with the brown sugar, those are the two main ingredients. But this will do," she said, reaching for a tub of runny margarine.

I leaned my head on my hand, inhaling the smell of garlic and onions frying in the cast iron skillet. I was so tired I was almost dropping off.

For two weeks we had been up at six, out on the colonies all day, and compiling notes after dinner. Each night I fell into bed, my limbs heavy as stone, and was instantly engulfed in dreams, epics with casts of family and friends. The sound of the sea was a roaring crowd, an engine. Night after night I dreamed of aircraft—helicopters circled as if to land then flew off; a huge jet carved three loops over the island and crashed into flames on our beach. In the morning I woke still tired.

I looked over at Anne, carefully measuring a cup of sugar. Suddenly, I was exhausted by her obsession with her work. I was trapped, ensnared by my own foolish fantasies of life on an enchanted island.

My misery must have shown on my face—she pushed her sleeves up, began beating the mixture with a wooden spoon, and glanced over at me. "Let's take a day off tomorrow," she said.

When the sun shone, the wind must have feared we would be

Part One

seduced into loving this place, for it blew fiercely. The sea was mussel blue, corniced with white crests. I carried a bucket to the shore and filled it with seawater to heat on the wood stove. Throwing a handful of dry soap in with socks, jeans, and T-shirts, I plunged my hands in, rubbing the clothes together to remove caked guano and mud. Then I carried them back to a tide pool to rinse them. We had become miserly with fresh water, since we had to carry every drop down the long beach.

When I finished I laid my clothes out on beach logs. They would dry quickly today. But on the first rainy day they would become damp, the salt residue absorbing moisture. I looked sadly at the ragged remains of my scarlet flannel shirt. Last week it had been my last clean one. I put it on in the morning and set off for a day of work. At lunch I noticed a hole near the hem. By late afternoon I noticed another hole, not a tear or a burn. By the end of the day the bottom half of the shirt had disappeared, apparently into thin air. Baffled, I searched my mind, then I remembered hauling the radio battery down the beach in my pack, padded on the bottom with my favourite shirt. Battery acid had soaked into it. Warmed by my body heat, it had eaten the fabric. I cursed the radio anew.

I pinned my laundry down with stones, and wedging myself behind a log out of the wind, spread my hands in my lap to warm. My fingers were red from the frigid water, cracked around the nails from salt and digging in puffin burrows. A dirty Band-Aid was wrapped around one finger where I cut it prying keyhole limpets off rocks to add to yesterday's dinner. I turned my face to the sun, savouring the feeling of being alone. Despite my loneliness, I had almost no time to myself. The waves sighed, the sea looked almost tropical blue. I ran my fingers through my lank hair, stripped off my clothes and picked my way over the slippery tideline.

My feet were numb by the time I was up to my knees in water. Standing naked in the wind, I felt as exposed as a clam without its shell, soft and white, and completely ill-adapted to this cold shore. When I was waist deep, I could bear it no longer. I dove in, instantaneously shooting back up breathless, and stumbled back to the shore, my head aching and my skin on fire.

Fumbling into my clothes with clumsy hands, I dressed as quickly as I could and lay on my stomach, pressing myself against the warm stones. Between the stones was a grit of shell shards. I sifted through them idly, picking complete shells out and lining them up: tiny orange swimming scallops, pale pink clams no bigger than a baby's fingernail, coiled snail shells ringed exquisitely with gold and purple, nacreous fragments of abalone and mussel. When the Europeans first arrived on this coast they described the pierced nasal septa of Native noblewomen hung with abalone ornaments. Men used mussel shells as tweezers to pluck their naturally sparse facial hair.

I found a small clam shell, white as talc, with a perfectly round hole in its base, the work of a predatory whelk. To get at the tender clam flesh, the snail's tough rasping mouth parts drilled into the shell and destroyed the muscle that held it shut. I removed one of my gold earrings and hung the clam shell on it.

I got up, shook my stiff limbs, picked up my pack and walked on. The familiar soundtrack of the beach—the staccato whistles of oystercatchers—rose and fell above the surf. I glanced over at the band of birds where they gathered on the rocks preening and lounging. They were crow-sized, black with long, lipstick-red beaks, and legs like old men in shorts—pale pink and knobby-kneed.

Oystercatchers call to each other constantly, drawing out territories and announcing their arrival to their mates or the group. I didn't notice the ascending urgency of whistles until I finally looked up from my daydreams to find a bird a few yards away, limping and crouching. I stopped and examined the ground carefully. The oystercatcher continued its frantic keening. I saw nothing. Just as I decided that it was overreacting, I looked near my right foot. A boot-length away was the bird's shallow "scrape" or nest. Lying in the centre were three eggs, greyish white with dark speckles. They looked exactly like granite beach stones. I apologized profusely to the oystercatcher and walked away quickly. The nest was only a few yards from the high-tide line. It was lined with a handful of bleached white shell fragments, for insulation and possibly to reflect the sun and keep the eggs from overheating. I moved down the beach and sat almost out of sight, pulling my sketchbook out to draw them. The mate arrived. They called to each other, stiffening and bowing, then the second bird walked a meandering route to the nest, as if preoccupied with other matters, crouched, and settled silently on the eggs.

I continued to the end of the beach, turned the corner marked by strands of dark reef and stepped onto the west beach. The wind atomized the crests of breaking rollers, sweeping spray a hundred feet up and spinning it into a gauzy veil of salt mist. I wondered where these waves were born. Trains of waves can travel thousands of miles if they do not meet hostile winds or land. In the southern oceans, the westerlies drive swells that roll around the globe, unimpeded by land, creating some of the longest waves in the world. Some summer waves breaking on the west coast of North America have been traced from these waters.

Today's waves looked young, only recently molded by wind—a rapid succession of peaks, spilling foam down their steep faces. Perhaps they were swollen by powerful tidal streams off the shores of Triangle Island—the bankless rivers formed by tides sweeping around land, over underwater canyons. The most dangerous waters in the world are created when great waves, born of storms far at sea, slam into tidal streams like this.

I watched wave after wave. The swells rose like the backs of sea creatures about to emerge, the lips of the crests curling, glass green for an instant, before snarling into the shore. The beach was white with shattered shell and grains of sand. Embedded in it were rocks, smooth and sculpted, the half-buried scapulas and hipbones of giants.

May 29

Anne and I reluctantly agreed that it was time to deepen the pit toilet. The outhouse was a primitive structure, a short way down the beach from the trailer. Perched above the shallow hole were slivered planks to sit on, surrounded by three walls of grey weathered cedar. The open side faced the slope, robbing the occupant of the view, but providing privacy and rickety protection from the southeast storms.

I climbed down the edge of the chest-deep pit in my gumboots and began shovelling to one side the residue left by several summers

of seabird biologists. I had to admit this was not what I pictured, a few months ago, imagining my work on Triangle Island.

"At least the ground is soft," I said grudgingly, as we hit fresh soil.

In fact, as I looked more closely, it was completely unlike the rocky soil in my garden at home. It was full of shells. I bent over and picked out a fragment of clamshell. It was blackened and snapped easily, a sign that it had been cooked in a fire. The next shovels of earth yielded more clams, as well as mussels and bone fragments. We were digging through midden—ancient rubbish heaps.

I leaned on my shovel for a moment and squinted through the cedar slats to the deserted beach, trying to imagine the flash of paddles above canoes. Was this shore, this hard fist of stone, once home?

All that was left were these shovels of shell and bone. The land once known as *wadi*—"where the spring never runs dry"—bore no shadows of its people; the ghosts had been carried off by the tide, swept away by the wind and rain. Almost nothing is known of them, except that they were probably never a large tribe. By the time of the first major census on this coast in 1838, they numbered only seventy-five. Within a few years they disappeared from the islands forever.

The Scott Islands are part of the Kwakiutl (or Kwakwaka'wakw) traditional territories. The Yutlinuk, a tribe of the Kwakiutl, moved easily among these islands in canoes hewn from the massive cedars of Vancouver Island. Summers were rich with harvests of birds and eggs. During the winters they crossed perilous straits to visit neighbouring villages for winter ceremonies and potlatches. They brought with them gifts of puffin beaks, bright rattles sewn onto ritual aprons for the songs and dances that each noble family performed. In the dim light of the bighouse, story cycles embellished with costumes and elaborate masks spun into the long rainy nights. Man-eating spirits came to life; women gave birth to frogs, made birds fly and caused the moon to wax and wane; dancers slipped into the shapes of wolves, bears, eagles and ravens.

By the 1950s, when the anthropologist Wilson Duff travelled to the Scott Islands with Mungo Martin, a renowned Kwakiutl carver, the only sign of the Yutlinuk was an old village site on

Lanz, one of the wooded islands to the east of Triangle. Only a graveyard, middens and moss-covered paddles kept the memory of these people from disappearing forever.

When we finished our digging I walked down to the sea to rinse my boots, wading ankle-deep into a tide pool. I scanned the dark bulbs of kelp swaying off shore, hoping for a sea otter. Nothing moved except the gulls circling above. I thought of a Kwakiutl sea otter mask used in one of the important winter dances, the Siwidi story cycle. Kumugwe, the chief of the undersea kingdom, takes the boy Siwidi, into the underwater world and gives him special knowledge and powers. One of the many forms the hero takes before returning to the world of humans is a sea otter. Four upward curving arms crowned with gulls surround the otter mask. Pull a string coiled at its base and the arms spin like a child's top, sending the gulls in circles, their cloth wings flapping.

But what seems timeless can change. The oral stories with which the Kwakiutl wove order out of the chaos of existence, were almost lost in one generation. Just as fragile was the story of the otters that once lived in numbers among these islands.

A book on the shelf in our trailer described two British ships under the command of James Cook, making their way towards the promising opening of an inlet, on March 28, 1778. As they threaded a wide swath of kelp which broke the swell, still massive from southeast storms, the travel-weary men may have seen lithe animals with whiskered faces and bright black eyes. Lying on their backs among the glistening, olive-green blades, the creatures would have amused the sailors with their human qualities, as they pulled their baggy skins this way and that to rub their lustrous brown coats with their front and hind feet, squeezing them between their forepaws. The sailors could never have guessed that these creatures bore the thickest fur of any living animal, with over 20,000 hairs in a patch of skin the size of a fingernail. As the animals churned the water around them into a froth or blew into their fur, they were finishing essential, meticulous grooming. Unlike the sea lions and seals common in these waters, sea otters do not have blubber for insulation, but rely on their fur to keep them warm.

Leaving the otters in the swaying kelp, the ships, the *Resolution*

Part One

and *Discovery*, nudged their way into a vast bay, protected from the open sea and mantled with dark forest. Yuquot, the anchorage they found in what is now called Nootka Sound, was studded with islands, overwhelmed by snow-topped mountains and fed by pure streams. Shortly after they arrived a group of Natives paddled out to meet them. One young officer recorded in his journal:

> We were surrounded by 30 or 40 [canoes]. It will require the assistance of one's imagination to have an adequate idea of the wild, savage appearance and actions of these first visitors, as it is difficult to describe the effect of gestures and motions. Their dark, copper-coloured bodies were so covered over with filth as to make it a doubt what was really the proper colour; their faces were daubed with red and black paint and grease, in no regular manner, but as their fancies led them; their hair was clotted also with dirt, and to make themselves either fine or frightful, many put on their hair the down of young birds, or plaited it in seaweed or thin strips of bark dyed red…

I formed a cup with my hands, scooped cold water and splashed it on my forehead, running it back over my tangled hair, tied back with an old red shoelace I had picked up on the beach. The other day I had been surprised by my own image in our small, salt-stained mirror: sun-bleached strands at my temples twisting out of my dark hair, the whites of my eyes startling in my tanned face.

I looked across the water toward the pale blue shadow of Vancouver Island, where Cook and his men found refuge from spring storms, sailing into the territories of the people who occupied lands just to the south of the Kwakiutl, the Nootka (or Nu-chah-nulth). Like the Kwakiutl, the Nootka harvested seafood and salmon, but they were more seafaring and were fearless whalers. They also hunted the docile sea otter. The chiefs would have arrived to meet Cook and his men dressed in sea otter cloaks, which they wore only on extraordinary occasions. During the month the British traded sea otter pelts for iron and other metals.

Seven years after Cook left, the first trading ship arrived at Nootka Sound. As the maritime fur trade picked up momentum,

the outhouse

Nootka became a major trading port. Boats from Great Britain, Russia, the United States and Spain converged on the northwest coast. In those early years of the sea otter trade, traditional Native life changed little. The Europeans were at a disadvantage, having come a long way for something they could get only from the locals. Trade, largely controlled by Natives, was for the most part peaceful. Otters became scarcer and conflicts arose between Europeans and Natives, and among Native groups competing for trade. As the otter population declined, the value of their fur increased. By the time they were protected, in the early part of this century, over a million sea otters had been taken from the region; only 1,000 to 2,000 remained from the Kuril Islands to California. The coat they developed to survive had turned out to be a deadly asset.

The disappearance of sea otters changed the face of the coast in unexpected ways. The kelp forests, which once ran along the exposed coast in thick ribbons, hundreds of miles long, diminished.

Sea otters need to eat a quarter of their body weight each day to generate enough heat to stay warm. They satisfy this voracious appetite with foods like abalone and snails; they break urchins with club-like paws or dive down to find a rock which fits their dexterous forepaws, lie on their backs and bang at them until they open. The kelp beds' sinuous canopies of dappled light provide shelter, food and spawning grounds for complex communities of fish, crabs, snails and other creatures. In many areas these were the otter's feeding grounds. With the otters' demise, populations of these animals, especially sea urchins, exploded. Like herds of marine cattle, urchins now moved over the sea floor, grazing the young kelp and other seaweeds from the rocky bottom. The ecology of the kelp forests was profoundly altered.

I lingered for a few more moments at the edge of the sea, listening to the water slap my rubber boots. The kelp lay motionless on the breast of the bay, which rose and fell in long slow breaths. A few years ago, eighty-nine sea otters from Alaska were flown into a bay on the west coast of Vancouver Island. The population was growing slowly; the kelp forests where they live were becoming richer in species and more complex in structure. But they had not yet returned to Triangle Island. The beds that once cradled otters were empty.

June 1

A bright, hard northwest wind had been blowing for days, polishing the sky like a blue stone. As we walked the beach after a day of work, a boat steamed into the bay. The crew lowered a tiny rowboat over the side. Three men climbed down into it and rowed through the kelp, huddled like beetles on a leaf, dodging surf and rocks. I tensed as they approached the shore, waiting for the wave that would overturn them. One leapt out and pulled on the bow, chased by surf that buried him up to his knees. He cursed loudly, while the others laughed and jumped onto the beach, slipping over seaweed in a scramble for dry land. They were dressed in jeans, shirtsleeves and black leather slip-on ankle boots. The fact that most fishermen never wore sensible boots and waterproof clothing was a mystery to me.

When the boat was tied up, they stood looking up and down the long beach, as if deciding which direction to walk, and noticed us for the first time. "Hello!" I called into the wind, waving. I could smell cigarette smoke.

A week ago, Anne and I were surprised when a fish boat dropped anchor in the bay. Two fishermen rowed ashore in the evening and Anne and I walked to the beach to meet them. I was so excited to see other human beings that I had to make an effort not to run, throw my arms around them and breathlessly ask them a million questions. Not expecting to find anyone here, let alone two young women, they looked like they had seen ghosts. We had chatted about the weather, the news and fishing. They were fishing farther out than most salmon boats venture, in search of halibut. They asked us about our work. "Don't you get lonely out here, by yourselves?" one said.

"No, we're too busy," Anne answered.

I smiled wanly. Before they left, we gave them letters to post. Anne's was addressed to her family, mine to Steven.

I was curious about what this group would have to say.

"So, you're the girls we heard about." A short, stocky man stamped out a cigarette on the beach. I glanced from one man to another and back at Anne, who was a few steps behind me. For a brief moment I was nervous. Then the man smiled self-consciously. "Thought we'd stretch our legs, and drop off a couple of things for you." He held up a plastic shopping bag.

Fishermen spend long evenings talking on the radio. They speak to their wives and girlfriends. With each other they discuss their fishing success, in veiled codes and aphorisms, which could be tips for buddies or red herrings for rivals. And they gossip. News of the biologists on Triangle Island had travelled fast.

I thanked him and took the bag, holding it open and peering into it at coffee, bread and a great slab of halibut, its skin darkly speckled, its dense flesh white as milk. The meat had been cut from just in front of the tail. Judging from its size, the fish must have been enormous. Pacific halibut can grow to weigh many hundreds of pounds, so large that they are dangerous when pulled out of the water. I wondered how long this fish had lived patiently pressed against the glacial gravels around Triangle Island. It could have been older than my grandmother. I felt regret as I gazed down at the delicately mottled flank. But it was fleeting. It was weeks since we had tasted fresh meat, and halibut is delicious.

I thanked the man and introduced myself. "Gary," he said, shaking my hand, then jamming his into his jean pocket. Anne stepped forward and looked into the bag. Her eyes lit up when she saw the coffee. We were down to a cup every two days. She asked Gary about the birds they saw on the fishing grounds, and I turned to the other two men, pointing out the trail they could walk to the next beach.

As we turned to carry our booty back to the trailer, Gary slipped a package of chocolate covered raisins out of his pocket and tossed them in the bag. "Okay then, we'll see you tomorrow," he said.

I looked at Anne, surprised. "They'll take us offshore tomorrow," she answered.

It was sometimes difficult to tell when Anne was excited about something. She didn't laugh uproariously or talk with her hands. But I knew she was thrilled. She had mentioned many times, as we looked out over the waters beyond the island, how little was known about most seabirds' lives when they were at sea. "Maybe we'll get to see where puffins fish," she smiled.

June 2

The next morning, we stood on the beach, under a colourless lid of sky, while Gary rowed the skiff in to pick us up. The boat was a wooden troller—like almost every small fish boat on the coast, practical, unpretentious and built to weather almost anything the Pacific threw at it. It had a wide, gently curving hull, a high pointed bow, a square stern, and a squat, cozy wheelhouse. Long metal poles extended above its roof, like silver antennae. During fishing these are extended outwards, to hang the lines from.

"Tom there will show you around below," said Gary as he began to winch up the anchor. One of the crew we had met on the beach, a shy, wiry man in his early twenties, led the way down a narrow companionway to a tiny galley smelling of coffee and diesel. Mid-ship were bunks and behind that a sealed fish hold.

As we climbed back up on deck, Tom handed up two steaming cups of coffee. I gave one to Anne and passed along the powdered creamer that followed. Looking for a place to sit on the deck, I spied a big, square lid. "Okay if I sit here?" I asked Tom when he emerged from the galley.

"Long as the fish don't mind," he said with a faint smile.

"Can I see them?" I asked.

He lifted the fibreglass lid. The hold was a dim cave where a half-dozen halibut, laid out on white shelves of ice, leered up at me. Several of them probably weighed twice as much as me. I had never seen a whole halibut before. Shy bottom dwellers, they survive, quietly blending into the sea floor, as if driven into hiding by their grotesque faces.

Halibut belong to a group of fish called righteye flounders—not to be confused with lefteye flounders. They are born with a symmetrical body and an eye on each side of their head, and for a time they swim around like any other fish. One day, though, they begin to change. Their left eye slowly begins to migrate to the right side of their head, the skull twisting with it. The fish swims in an ever more drunken tilt and the upper side of the body darkens to the colour of stone. When the transformation is complete the halibut drifts to the bottom, settling on its pale, sightless side, its bulging, wall eyes jammed above a contorted grin.

Part One

When they are home they move little, but once a year they slide into deep waters and migrate. They travel fast, a wedge of muscle moving through darkness for hundreds of miles, until they reach the Gulf of Alaska, where they spawn. By early spring they are back again.

"Looks like a good haul so far," I said as he lowered the lid.

"Have to get a few more before we head home," he shrugged.

I was just about to ask how many fish they needed to make a fishing trip pay when the anchor came up. Tom went forward to help secure it. I sat down and began to drink the industrial-strength brew from my chipped mug. The horizon swung around and we headed out of our bay.

The mood on the boat was festive. The men had been out for a week, getting up before dawn, fishing until dusk. This was a day off.

We circled the island, hugging the eastern shore, so fortified with rock walls and cliffs we had not been able to walk it. Anne scanned carefully for puffins with her binoculars. A rank, fishy smell drifted toward us. On a small islet, a group of male sea lions lifted their heads and jostled each other nervously. The animals highest on the rock were biggest. Their fur was pale gold—making them look, from a distance, like weathered logs, tossed high. As we passed, the largest male roared and the others joined in a belching chorus.

We rounded a point, crowned with a tall pinnacle of dark rock and saw the shore of North Bay, with its rail tracks scarring the island's flank. Huge swells, spawned by the recent wind, collapsed on the beach. The boat parted the waves. Little groups of common murres, sleek, black and white birds that nested on Triangle's rock faces, scattered at our bow, rowing awkwardly away through the water with their stiff wings.

We turned south, the boat suddenly dwarfed by cliffs, and found ourselves looking into the great hole in Puffin Rock. Past daylight at the entrance, the water was dark. Far off, at the end of the tunnel, we saw a piece of sky. A roar echoed off the stone amphitheatre. I shuddered when I thought of a story a biologist who had worked here told me. He and some visiting filmmakers had decided to take an inflatable Zodiac with a tiny engine through the maelstrom. Halfway in, they were thrown against rock and tore a hole in the bottom. They almost sank before they retreated and beached on the nearest shore for repairs.

The angry ocean poured through the hole, trapped like a genie in a bottle. I could understand why it had found its way into Native story. It was the origin of the mythic and terrifying cannibal for the Nakomgilisala, the Kwakiutl people who looked out at the Scott Islands from the northwest tip of Vancouver Island.

I had read about the cannibal in a book by Franz Boas, the American anthropologist who recorded what he could learn of coastal cultures a hundred years ago. The cannibal is one of the strangest and most important characters in the winter dances of the Kwakiutl. The cannibal dance or *hamatsa* was an initiation ritual. A young male was secluded in the woods and taught the long dance cycle. Then he performed it in the longhouse playing the role of a cannibal, biting people and appearing to cut off pieces of flesh, attended by cannibal birds—dancers wearing heavy masks armed with beaks more than a yard long. As the bird dancers pulled the secret strings of their masks they called "yap, yap," and snapped the beaks, with which in myth they broke the skulls of human beings and ate their brains.

As Gary turned the wheel and we swung away from Puffin Rock and out to sea I looked back. A cormorant flew out of the mouth of the hole, its black feathers gleaming, trailing darkness.

The bow lifted and fell, slicing through a ten-foot swell. Behind the boat, the water knit itself back together, barely leaving a wake. Triangle grew smaller and slipped into the sea. Groups of murres and cormorants thinned and disappeared. Solitary puffins dove when we passed, more shy of us on the water than on land. At about ten miles out we saw the last of them. The wind picked up and I fought the first flutters of seasickness. Trying to calm the small, chaotic sea of coffee in my stomach, I fixed my eyes on the horizon. I stared at its faint line scoring the seamless grey of water and sky, until it began to transform, billowing up in a misty plume. I blinked and refocussed my eyes. The plume faded slowly, but nearby, another bloomed. "Whales!" I shouted. Anne whirled around to where I was pointing, and peered through her binoculars. Forgetting my seasickness

Part One

I jumped up and scrambled to the wheelhouse, grabbing at lines and railings to steady myself.

Gary was leaning over the wheel, watching the sea absent-mindedly. He looked more relaxed behind the wheel of the boat than on land, but he did not miss much. By the time I reached him he had nudged the spoke gently with his elbow. The boat was already heading for the blows.

Anne and I had sighted whales before. With our bird's eye view from the island we had seen the low, indistinct blow and brief slice of black fin of a minke, the smallest of the baleen whales. Another time we had watched an adult and a young whale blow several times. Their low, humped dorsal fins slowly curled out of the water, followed by tail flukes waving like huge hands, before they slipped under in a long, deep dive. They were humpbacks, probably a mother and calf, that had migrated from wintering grounds in Hawaii or Mexico. In those warm, shallow waters females give birth and males court, hanging upside down like great bells, ringing with song. There is little food in tropical waters and by the time they reach the north Pacific, the adults have not eaten for many months. Fattening each summer on the north Pacific's buffet of krill and schooling fish like herring, capelin and sandlance, humpbacks are able to endure months of winter fasting.

The spouts ahead of us today were different. They rose in tall columns, opening into a canopy of spray the size of a small tree. Gary slowed to a few knots and the boat rocked, the rigging drawing woozy arcs across the sky. With two whales farther off, we approached the closest spout. Suddenly, about three boat lengths away from us a dark shape rose out of the water. Gary punched the boat into neutral and we slowed as the animal blew. Anne and I clambered to the bow, looking down at the surfacing wedge of a very large whale head, just yards away. We could see the characteristic double blowholes of a baleen whale. They were the size of plates. A cloud of fishy-smelling vapour drifted over us and we heard the deep whistle of air intake. The whale began to sink, rolling slightly, as if trying to get a look at us. For a moment I thought I saw the faint gleam of a small, dark eye. The pale underside of the jaw and pleated throat shimmered before he began a shallow dive. The dark curve of back seemed to never end. Finally a scimitar of dorsal fin appeared and the animal submerged. He surfaced less than a minute later not far away, but on the other side of the boat. To our surprise when the head rose, we could not see a white throat. I dug the dog-eared *Whales of Canada* out of my raincoat pocket—though we were looking for birds, I had hoped we might see whales and had grabbed it as we left that morning.

"Anne," I said, "this has got to be a fin whale."

We bent over the description of the whale, second only to the blue in size: "Fin whales show one of the strangest asymmetries in the animal world: the lower part of the right side of the head is white, while the left is grey." Even the tongue and baleen of fin whales are harlequin: the front baleen plates on the right side are white, but the rest are striped with bands of yellowish white and bluish grey. Meanwhile the asymmetry is reversed on the tongue, grey on the right side, white on the left. The rest of the whale's colouring is typical of many marine creatures, adapted to live in a world that is top-lit—grey on the back and sides, and white below. It went on to explain that this "countershading" might be useful when fishing. The fin whale sometimes circles a school of fish, turning on its side as it opens its mouth. The dark might be used as camouflage, the white to flash and "startle" or "herd" the fish.

We stayed with the whale as it dove a few more times, almost lazily, then arched its back steeply and disappeared, leaving nothing but a great circle of dimpled water, a "whale print," which the waves quickly erased. We knew that it would be a while before we saw him again. Fin whales could dive deeper than the hundred fathoms of seawater below us. And they could stay under for almost half an hour.

I wondered if the whale was "talking" or listening to his two farther companions. Even if we had a hydrophone to dangle over the rail of the boat into the water, we could not eavesdrop on their conversation. Humans cannot hear the wavelengths of their language. Fin whales make deep-throated moans of about twenty hertz, which last about a second. Twenty hertz lies at the very bottom of the sounds we can hear when we are young children.

sea stars: low tide

different colour phases of the same species: *Pisaster ochraceus*

Fin whales make trains of moans, spaced with several seconds. The sounds of the fin whale, along with those of the blue whales (which make similar but longer moans) are the loudest and lowest sounds of any animals. If we could hear them, it would be like standing beside the runway as a 747 takes off.

When these sounds were first recorded, they were so regular, loud and low, they were thought to be amplifier malfunction. When this proved wrong, it was suggested that the sounds were seismic signals from inside the earth, or breaking surf on the shores of continents. Finally, someone suggested that the Russians were filling the oceans with low-frequency sounds that would allow them to track US submarines. Money poured in for research. As soon as it was discovered that they came from fin whales, the funds dried up, but not before whale biologists calculated that, before ship traffic, fin whale song could have travelled as far as 4,000 miles and still be heard against the normal background noise of the sea.

Animals that range widely over the open ocean face the dilemma of how to find each other. Most, from puffins and sea lions, to sea turtles and salmon, solve it by congregating in breeding grounds. But this can be costly. Whales like humpbacks and greys were decimated on breeding grounds. Whalers never found a breeding ground for fin and blue whales. Acoustic tracking of whales has confirmed that whale sound can travel very long distances. Fin whales, dispersed thinly in the seas, probably find each other in something similar to an oceanic telephone dating service, by listening over hundreds or thousands of miles for each other.

What would it be like to experience the world through sound? Was the voice of a mate a sensuous curve? Was a school of fish a silver cascade? Did the sonar of a killer whale cast a terrifying shadow?

As the spouts faded in the distance, I noticed my queasiness again. I left Anne in the bow and made my way amidships, to the most stable part of the boat. Gary revved up once more and we were soon motoring at a steady nine knots, the engine purring and puffing diesel exhaust. For many miles the ocean was empty. If we kept going, pointed out to sea, by nightfall we would drop off the edge of the world: the continental shelf would plunge into

Part One

the abyss. Just as I was sure that we must have left all life behind, Anne called from the bow. A black smudge like smoke trailed, eclipsed every few seconds in the troughs of swell. Gradually the dark line resolved into a stream of birds slightly bigger than gulls, gliding just above the water.

They seemed to ride a magic carpet, flying just above the water, their narrow wing tips almost touching the waves. The flock unravelled for miles. Tens of thousands of sooty shearwaters passed like spirits, silently slicing through the air twice as fast as our boat, rarely flapping their wings.

Though seabirds make up only about three percent of the 8,600 known species of birds in the world, as individuals they far outnumber land birds. Shearwaters are the most common birds in the world. But most people never see them. Over a billion shearwaters of several species spend their lives at sea or on remote islands. When they have finished nesting in burrows on South American and Australasian islands, they turn north, traversing whole oceans. Fifty million shearwaters alight in the north Pacific summer to fatten on schooling fish, squid and tiny shrimp.

The last birds overtook us. One remained on the horizon, resolutely separate. It was flying very fast, on unflapping wings, like the shearwaters. I fought the peculiar apathy of seasickness, forcing myself to pick up my binoculars. "Anne," I said, "what do you think that is?" I was afraid that if I said what I suspected before I was sure, my hopes would be dashed.

"It's 'uge!" she answered, forgetting, in her own excitement, to pronounce the "h."

It flew towards the stern of the boat where it circled and crossed, staying with us. Its wings were so long and narrow that it was hard to imagine how the bird could become airborne without a tow, like a glider.

"Hey, it's a gooney bird," Tom pointed.

Al, the other crew member, a small man with a weather-beaten face, was leaning on the rigging. He grinned, "Yeah, they follow us all the time, waiting for us to throw them scraps. They're real garbage-guts; they'll eat almost anything." He looked over at us mischievously, checking to see how this went over.

I flipped through my bird book to albatross. Sailors and

fishermen had their own affectionate names for most seabirds: puffins were "sea parrots," the tiniest auks, murrelets were "kiss-me-arses" for their habit of diving so quickly that the only thing you saw was their back end, just before they disappeared. "Gooney bird" was their name for albatross.

My book confirmed that albatross, being mostly surface feeders, will pick up fish offal as well as garbage, even popcorn thrown off the back of boats. Sometimes they also eat plastic and aluminum. Two birds washed up on the west coast of Vancouver Island contained seventeen man-made objects in their stomachs!

Tom was finishing a ham and cheese sandwich. The smell of mustard made me more nauseous. He tossed the crust overboard.

The albatross veered off and landed, folding its origami wings into its sides. It sat on the water like a duck in a city pond gobbling up bread tossed by Sunday picnickers.

I watched the bird, its mystique untarnished by its silly name or scavenging. It was a black-footed albatross and had soared here on wings spanning over seven feet. It was probably born on one of the northwestern Hawaiian islands, like Midway, and may have been wandering the oceans for years, waiting until it was old enough to breed. The birds sometimes return to the island at three or four years of age, but not until they are about nine do they choose the mate they will keep for life, courting with elaborate dances, bowing and bill snapping. Or it could have a chick there now, waiting for it to return with a bellyful of food.

By May, black-footed albatross chicks are about half grown. The ultimate working parents, albatross don't even see each other when they are sharing feeding duties. One arrives to deliver up to a quart of regurgitated fish and squid to its single, big chick, while the other is out at sea, fishing for the next delivery. In round trips that can take three weeks, black-footed albatross routinely cover vast distances in the Pacific, flying to the rich, temperate waters on the continental shelves, both to the west and east. Like shearwaters they frequent the roughest seas. The Latin root of the scientific order—Procellariformes—they are both placed in, along with fulmars and petrels, means "storm."

For a long time, just how albatross soared without the thermals and updrafts that sustain birds over land was a mystery. Design-wise, albatross couldn't be more different from puffins.

In flight, auks' small wings bear the burden of their relatively large bodies. Birds like murres have the highest burden, or "wing loading" of any flying birds. To stay aloft they must flap like crazy. With long wings that are only about six inches wide, albatross have the lowest wing loading. Providing there is some wind, once they get their spindly contraption aloft, they can glide almost forever, with hardly a flap.

The other secret of albatross flight has to do with the nature of ocean wind. The wind just over the water is slowed by friction. Above this it is more rapid. Albatross ride the fast upper wind, losing height and gaining momentum. When they hit the slower layer they use this momentum to turn into the wind and climb back up. Then they once more turn and ride downward, with the wind at their backs. Gliding at thirty knots, the albatross, day after day, does what only the fastest sailboats, like the Whitbread and America's Cup craft, can do with an expert crew under ideal conditions.

The albatross faced the wind, unfolded its wings and ran for many yards, its webbed feet slapping the water. Finally it lifted and began its circling flight. Effortlessly suspended, it seemed not so much to ride the wind as to create it, as if it were, as Coleridge's ancient mariner described it, "the bird that made the breeze to blow."

I looked around me, realizing that for the first time in my life I was out of sight of land. I had never imagined how empty the open ocean was. The surface was a one-way mirror below which life, moving through the water in perfect fluid casts, was hidden. Above was a desert of shifting liquid dunes, where living things were whittled away by wind. Many birds survived here by plundering the surface waters. But only the albatross seemed perfectly at home, a bird married to wind: wings worn smooth and long, instinct sharpened to the direction, speed, even the smell of the wind. Unlike most other birds, which are thought to have a poor sense of smell, albatross are believed to be able to detect distant scents like the subtle perfume, dimethyl sulfide, produced by plankton blooms. Albatross follow their noses to these fast food "fly-ins" where the plankton serves up smorgasbords of crustaceans, fish and squid.

As we turned back toward the island, travelling broadside to the waves, the boat rocked violently. Anne looked grim, her freckles dark against her pale skin. She watched the horizon with determination. I staggered to the leeward side of the boat, and heaved over the rail. Then, overcome with inertia, I stretched out on the deck and closed my eyes.

I didn't open them until we had dropped anchor in our bay. As I sat up I could hear the static of the radio. I stood up, still shaky. Anne wasn't on the deck. I found her in the wheelhouse and slumped into a seat next to her. She was talking to her supervisor about her research. It was beginning to look as if the number of gulls here, as opposed to puffin colonies in some other parts of the world, was small. Should she shift the focus of her study since there were not as many gulls as she had thought? He thought she should stick to her original research design for now. He was more worried about our radio and would try to send out a new one, along with some fresh supplies.

When she hung up, I gave the operator Steven's number, hopeful that this unexpected call would find him home.

"Hello." His familiar phone greeting was a statement, not a question. He had received my letter. I breathlessly recounted the first glimpse of the fin whale, the legions of shearwaters, the solitary albatross.

"It sounds like you're in such good spirits," he said, tentatively. I had forgotten that my letter had been full of doubts and loneliness. Today I had just returned from an exotic safari. I had seen creatures that live most of their lives unobserved, if not unaffected, by man. "Yeah," I said, "I'm okay."

June 3

Time changed shape. It became continuous and drew itself out to its full length. I lost track of the days and noticed only the progression of day and night. The island could not be placed in time, only in season—the season when light waxes and the birds return.

The north Pacific, wound up by the sun, ticks through its seasons, with the alarm set for spring, when the light lengthens and the seas calm.

Part One

The summer northwesterlies were beginning, pushing surface water into drifts that were twisted offshore by the rotation of the earth—the same Coriolis effect that stirs the earth's currents and winds into great circles. Cold water was welling up from below to replace the water flowing away from the coast, it blue tongues and shifting plumes meeting the warm, green surface, bringing dissolved minerals and nutrients that have been sealed in deep cold chambers. The effect was like throwing fertilizer on a lawn in the spring.

Suddenly a glass of seawater held up was milky with single-celled phytoplankton. The ones I could see were only the biggest, about a millimetre across. Unable to propel themselves they floated randomly across the light, like dust motes. Usually at the mercy of currents and winds—they are literally just what their Greek name means: "wandering" (*plagktos*) "plants" (*phuton*).

In our bay diatoms (phytoplankton whose bodies are encased in a pair of intricately patterned silica shells) were splitting in two every day—a single cell producing a million identical offspring every twenty days, each species their own intricate piece of glasswork: prongs and latticed spears, crowns of spines, floating flasks and pill boxes, vessels whorled like seashells or armoured like baroque helmets. They tumbled, uncountable, shearing light, spinning life into the ocean, turning the waters green and soupy.

On our nautical chart I read that the waters around the island were rarely over 50 fathoms deep. Triangle perches near the edge of the shallow shelf where continent wades up to its ankles in ocean. Her waters feel the contours and taste the flavours of the land. They wash over rocks once exposed to the sun, wind and rain, hills and valleys formed by glaciers, fans of sediments deposited by rivers; they are rich with minerals washed from the land and swept up by turbulent currents. Not far to the west of the island the shelf slips onto the sea floor, its slopes almost a mile high, steep and deeply cut in places with hidden grand canyons, scoured by rivers of sliding sediment.

Beyond lay different waters. Though leviathans fill the oceans of our imaginations, the open seas are biological deserts compared to the continental shelves. Below about 130 feet it's too dark for plants to photosynthesize. At 2,000 feet it's black as a locked box, and close to freezing. Life in these depths survives on the constant rain of dead plants and animals from above. Animals are studded with bioluminescence, winking and waving with cold flashes of chemical light. In the waters above, plants are unable to attach to anything. Unlike land plants, they do not grow into towering forms reaching towards the light. Most oceanic plants and animals are so small they cannot swim against the slow oceanic currents. Creatures like giant squid, basking sharks, and whales grow enormous, slowly mowing their way through ton after ton of tiny prey.

But in the rich meadows of phytoplankton blooming around our island, zooplankton grazed, some single-celled and others more complex: small transparent salps joined together in colonies a yard long, undulating flatworms, swimming crabs and vast numbers of tiny shrimp-like creatures. Other animals, the larvae of marine invertebrates, passed through the zooplankton community in temporary guises, looking nothing like their parents. A minute crab larva is an alien with a Quasimodo hunch, a barbed head and bulging "eyes." A barnacle larva begins life as a one-eyed, one-shelled microscopic animal with three pairs of legs.

Multitudes of larvae drifted or swam with beating cilia, or whip-like tentacles, feeding on other plankton and growing until they could find a place that felt like home: calm or turbulent water, a warm inlet, a sandy bottom, or wave-washed rock. Then they would settle and assume life in the familiar forms we knew: starfish, worms, barnacles, clams.

In the north Pacific a feeding frenzy was beginning. Sea lions and seals gorged themselves. Whales completed long migrations, from as far away as Hawaii, and the ocean swelled with over 30 million seabirds.

Like thousands of islands scattered over these waters, where the hem of the continent unravels, Triangle is a lifeboat far from shore, carrying creatures whose histories are woven into both land and sea.

By June every crack and crevice on the island was occupied: cormorant and murre eggs teetered on cliff ledges; gulls lay clutches in simple depressions on the ground; pigeon guillemots

concealed their eggs at the end of deep rock fissures. Puffins and auklets lay their eggs in the dark wombs of burrows. Cassin's auklets had already hatched.

Anne pulled a box marked "Canadian Wildlife Service" from under the table. She cut through tape with a blade, pried it open and began pulling out sheer folds of fabric.

I looked up from where I was sitting nearby, my hands covered with glue from trying to mend a hole in the ankle of one of my gumboots. I had forgotten about the sealed box as soon as I had stowed it away on our first day.

"What is that?" I asked.

"It's a mist net," she replied, as she struggled to untangle yards of the stuff on the tiny floor. "I can't do this here," she sighed in frustration. I wiped off my hands and followed her outside. As we opened the fine-meshed net over the beach logs, checking it for holes, Anne reminded me that we had to begin the first of several nights' work on the Cassin's auklet colonies. I remembered the contract she had with the wildlife service to collect food samples from the birds. We rolled up the net carefully.

Hours later, just before dusk, we hiked to the colonies on the western end of the island. We scoured the beach for long poles of driftwood, hauled them partway up the slopes and hung the nets from them. Anne braced her shoulder under one heavy timber, then the other, pushing them upright while I steadied them and tried to guide them into the holes we had dug in the loose earth. We piled stones around the bases and stepped back to look at our work. It looked like a makeshift soccer goal, the net sagging between precariously leaning posts. We settled in the grass, waiting for the game to begin.

The slopes to either side of us slid into gathering darkness. Blurred forms emerged from the direction of the sea. Somehow each parent knew how to find its chick on a hillside mined with hundreds of burrows. We heard the soft static of wings as they flew past us, straight into the ground, like souls flying into the underworld. The chicks welcomed them with muffled peeps.

A bird flew into our net with a muffled *whump*. We flicked on our headlights and Anne opened a Ziploc bag. I freed the struggling bird, caught like an insect in a spider web, by unlooping the delicate net from its flight feathers. It seemed to weigh no more

Part One

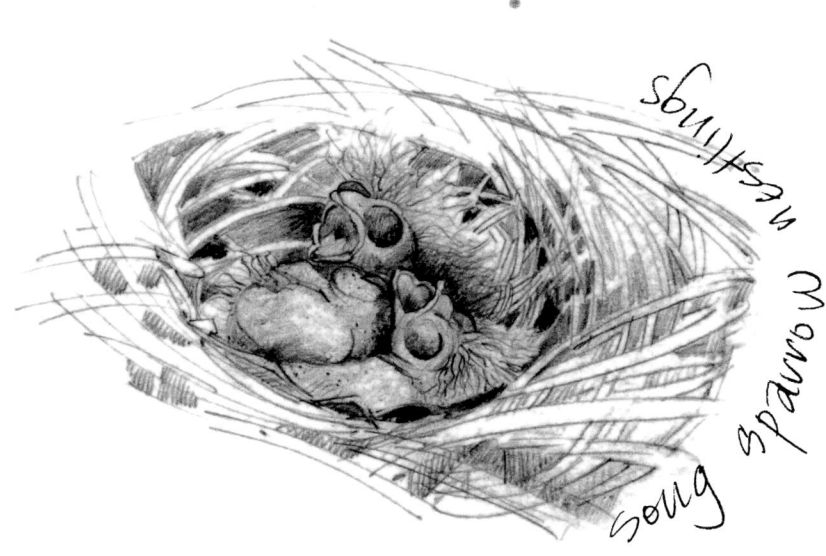

song sparrow nestlings

than a handful of down. I could feel its heart beating as I pinned back the wings and gently stroked its engorged throat. Out poured an oily, orange substance, which smelled like warm sardines. Anne fastened the bag and put it in her pack for weighing and preserving in formaldehyde. I stepped around the net and released the bird from the cage of my hands into the moonless dark.

The Cassin's auklets were returning from the sea, where they feed on zooplankton: copepods and euphausids, or "krill"—the tiny shrimp-like creatures that are a staple of the ocean's food chain. Whales harvest krill on massive baleen plates. Cassin's auklets tuck their catch into throat pouches for airlifting over miles of dark ocean to their hungry young.

As I sat down to wait for the next captive, I heard a hollow thud. I turned around. A bird had flown into one of the poles on which our net hung. When I found it in the grass it was already dead. I held it out to Anne. She took its krill sample and laid it back down.

I crouched and turned off my headlight, feeling as if I had

stolen this small life. I waited in the dark for the next bird, trying to reason with myself—a few losses in the pursuit of knowledge were part of research; collecting samples would help complete a study begun two years ago and perhaps illuminate the auklets' mysterious lives.

For centuries of summers, throngs of breeding seabirds had come here from the wilderness of the sea. In many parts of the world colonies were growing quiet. The birds were drowning in miles of fishing nets and becoming fouled from oil drilling and tanker traffic; fisheries were destroying their food sources. Their world was irrevocably caught up in the nets of our world. We would need all the knowledge we could gather to conserve them.

June 4

The puffin colonies were quiet. Pairs of lounging birds no longer dotted the slopes. At some burrow entrances one bird kept vigil; many more were deserted—egg laying had begun.

Incubating birds emerged and nuzzled their returning mates' beaks before stretching or flying off to feed. The partners stooped and disappeared into the burrows.

Feathers are such good insulators that a bird's body heat won't pass through them. Most birds develop areas of bare skin on their breasts during the breeding season. First they lose feathers, then the skin becomes so spongy and richly supplied with blood vessels it looks inflamed. When puffins incubate, they fluff up their breast feathers and apply one of two brood patches to the egg. A few Atlantic puffin pairs given an extra chick by researchers have managed to raise both. Occasionally an adult that loses its mate manages to rear a chick alone. But the chick's growth is always stunted and it usually dies. A single egg is the best clutch for a pair of puffins.

I crawled over the colonies, checking nests for eggs. If a bird had just left, the egg would be unattended. I slipped my bare hand—gloves were too clumsy—over the droppings smeared at the entrance, groping in the darkness. My fingers rested on something slimy, cold and wet. With a shiver I instinctively pulled them out before I remembered that slugs inhabited these burrows too.

Part One

The nest was a simple depression in the cool earth. No snug lining of down cradled the puffin's egg. A few strands of grass or a straggly feather or two were sometimes placed carelessly, as if the parent had had an inkling that it should prepare the nest in some way but got distracted. The creamy white egg was stained with smears of mud; it was about twice the size of a chicken egg, and rounder at the ends. Birds that lay eggs in dark places such as burrows or tree holes often lay white eggs, not needing protective markings and colorations. The eggs can be almost spherical, lacking the tapered end that prevents them from rolling out of a treetop or off a ledge.

I got out my calipers and measured the length and width of the egg, recording them with a pencil in a rain-stained notebook. Then I placed the egg in a cloth bag, folded over and suspended at the top with a clip attached to a hanging scale, and scribbled down the weight.

The egg was huge compared to the size of the bird. It was almost as long as my palm. Like many seabirds, tufted puffin females lay only one large egg. With a male to help incubate, the egg hatches into a robust chick. As long as the parents can deliver enough fish to it over the summer, it has a good chance of fledging (leaving the nest for the ocean as a full grown chick). But many birds, curled within the thousands of eggs in the catacombs, would not survive starvation and predation to return as breeding adults three or four years from now.

I carefully placed the egg back in the nest and moved on to the next burrow, gingerly extending my arm into the earth. I heard a low growl too late—my index finger was pinched hard by something that felt like needle-nosed pliers. I pulled my arm out lightning-quick and examined angry red marks left by the sharp beak. Rubbing them with my other hand, I stood up to move on to the next burrow, stepping carefully on narrow terraces of earth between clumps of tufted hairgrass so as not to damage the fragile terrain below me. I was almost at the edge of the colony when my heavy boot broke through the soil. I knelt down to repair it and saw yolk oozing into the dark earth. It was early enough in the season that this pair would probably lay again. But as I removed the broken eggshells and tossed them into the sea, I felt a hairline crack of guilt widen slightly.

As we began the trail down to the beach we heard the familiar thrum of a helicopter. It lifted over the eastern ridge of the island and landed far below in our small clearing. Through my binoculars I watched the rotors slow and stop. We scrambled down to investigate.

Anne's university supervisor had been as good as his word. The helicopter brought three boxes of fresh food—bread, cheese, meat, eggs, lettuce and tomatoes—and a new radio. We hurried back along the beach to exchange our old radio, in a wooden box covered with a tarp, at the base of Puffin Rock. The test run was perfect; the pilot climbed back into his helicopter.

He'll be back at the office in an hour, I thought to myself. Our remoteness suddenly dissolved. An hour away, people were sipping summer drinks on shady porches. Steven, just in from several days hiking, would be doing his washing and packing for his next expedition. I felt the sharp ache of absence. Only an hour away the world carried on, and yet, as the helicopter shrank to a tiny dot and disappeared into the distance, we were as far away as ever.

As if in confirmation, the new radio devised its own tricks. We trudged down the beach to sit by it at the appointed call time. It rang and I picked up the speaker.

"Hello, this is Triangle Island, over."

"I guess they're not answering their phone right now." It was Steven. He must have been told we had a new radio. Apparently, on his end, our phone was still ringing.

"Hello, hello!" I shouted into the mike. "Hello, we're here."

"Oh well, I'll try tomorrow."

I could still hear the disappointment in his voice as I trudged home, trying to console myself with the thought of a steak and crisp salad for dinner.

June 6

Anne called out from ahead of me on the beach. As I caught up with her I saw that she was holding a corpse, about the size of a chicken, with a long gawky neck and a potbelly. Its woolly grey down was wet and matted. It was an eaglet, less than half grown.

Part One

I touched the rough yellow talons and small, hooked beak—tiny replicas of the powerful weapons of the adult.

We squinted up at the nest above us—a platform of twigs, perched on a raised pinnacle on the ridge. In coastal forests, bald eagle nests sway 300 feet up in the broken tops of ancient Douglas fir or Sitka spruce. They can be as big as queen-sized beds and weigh more than two tons. On Triangle's barren flanks, the eagles chose the next best thing: a height of rock. The nest had beaches on two sides, dense seabird colonies nearby and a 360-degree view.

The eagles were already here when we came to the island in April. Had we been here in March we might have witnessed their courting, flying in mock pursuit of each other, or soaring in tightening circles until they came together, locking talons and tumbling freefall for a few, heart-stopping seconds through the air. We might have seen them searching the beach for sturdy twigs to add to the nest, stroking and pecking at each other's bills, or scanning the familiar vista in companionable silence. Chances are they knew this beach already and had nested here in previous years. Eagles appear to keep their mates, though new bonds can be made if pairs "divorce" after failed breeding, or if one dies.

In early spring the eagles on Triangle Island courted and waited for the arrival of 400,000 pairs of Cassin's auklets. As we had seen, auklets are a rich, but elusive, food supply—flying in after dark, leaving before light each morning, or remaining in the refuge of their burrows by day. Each day the eagles scoured the island for the sick or weak birds.

Soon after our arrival on Triangle Island, the activity at the nest suddenly ceased. The eagles were incubating, pressing themselves so low over the eggs that all we could see was a white head and tail. Incubation is a time of quiet co-operation for eagle pairs. One bird sits on the nest, the other searches for food. To relieve its mate, the returning bird moves carefully around the two or three creamy oval eggs, each about the size of a tennis ball. Clenching its feet so that the large hind claw is shielded by the front three toes—the equivalent of walking on its knuckles—it straddles the clutch, lowers its body and settles down with a subtle side-to-side rocking motion. About once an hour the sitter

VIEW FROM PUFFIN ROCK

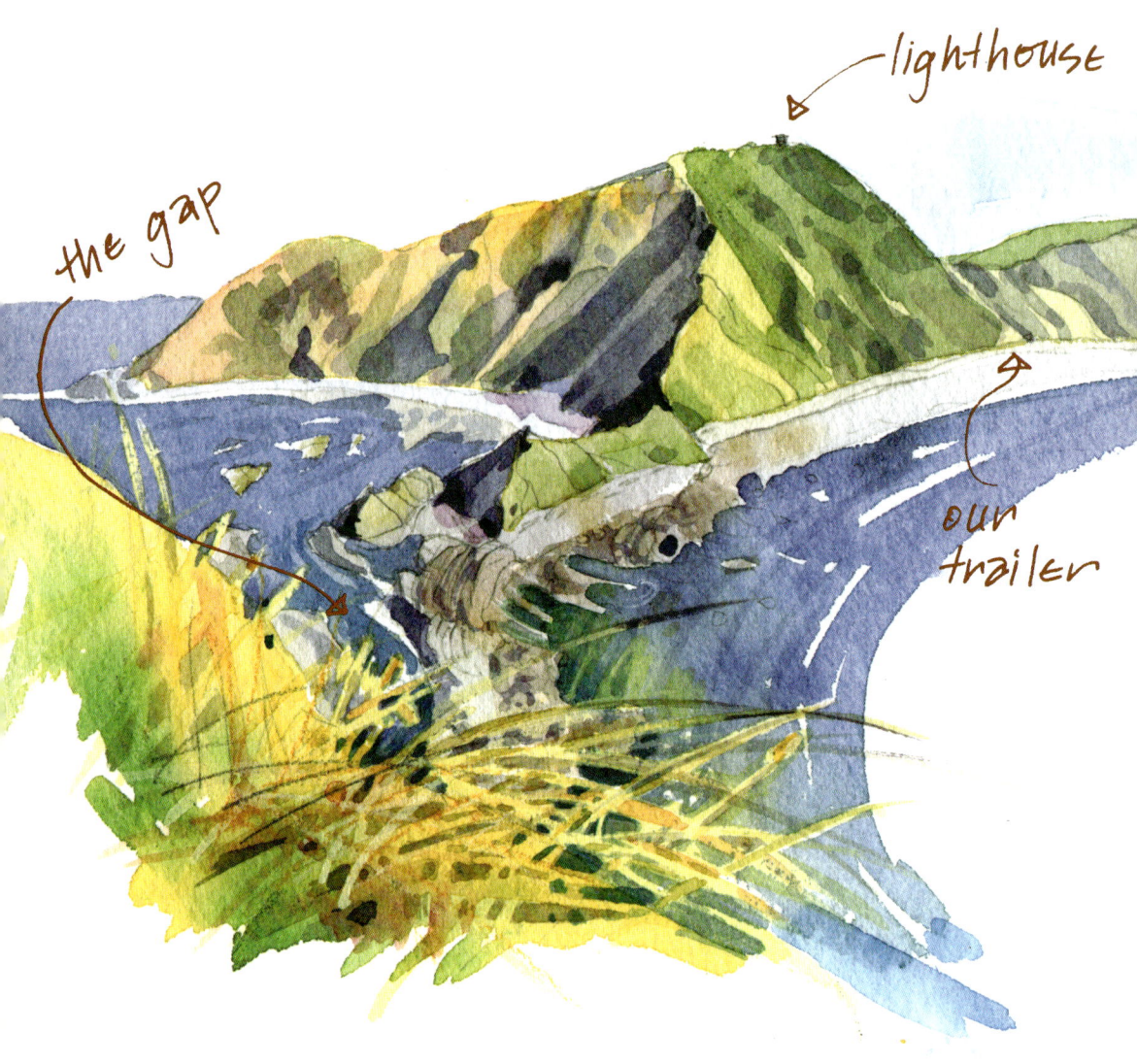

stands up, changes position or pokes around in the nesting material. This twenty-pound bird, with claws as long as a man's fingers and a beak that can tear flesh from bone, gently turns the egg to ensure even warming and to prevent the delicate membranes surrounding the embryo from sticking to the shell.

By mid-May we noticed the eagles sitting more upright. The eggs had hatched. The parents were brooding, tucking the chicks under their breasts. Both birds were soon making non-stop feeding trips to the nest, bearing small fish and dead birds. Over the weeks we watched the heads of the two eaglets emerge as they grew strong.

Now one was dead. How could it starve in this seabird smorgasbord? We decided to climb to the aerie to see if the other chick was still alive.

We walked to the base of the ridge through waist-high cow parsnip, the pungent, herbal smell of its crushed leaves rising around us. The climb quickly became a scramble up crumbling rock—pieces broke off and clattered to the bottom of the slope. About a hundred feet up, when we were just below the nest, an adult left its perch on the ridge above and swooped down, stretching and opening its talons. As its shadow passed over me, I heard the rush of wind through wings, and looked up at the six-foot span, a dark shape filling the sky.

"Anne, there must be a chick. Perhaps we shouldn't disturb it," I suggested. The adult gave a series of shrill, descending whistles and banked toward us again.

"But I didn't see the other chick's head from below," Anne called.

"Maybe he's sleeping," I offered weakly. The eagle let loose another ear-splitting call.

We climbed the last few feet and peered into the nest. It was an ogre's den, scattered with severed feet, wings, breastbones, and bleached vertebrae, and smelling of the rancid musky flesh of seabirds, the rankness of rotten fish. A cod head crawled with maggots. Except for these remains, it was empty.

The eagle swept so close to me I felt a few strands of my hair lift, just grazed by the outstretched hind claw. I ducked, gave Anne a wide-eyed look, and immediately started backing down the steep face. The eagle returned to its perch and fixed me with its yellow stare.

As I retreated, I tried to imagine what could have happened to the chicks, so healthy just a few days ago.

"Maybe they ate something toxic, or had a virus or parasite," Anne offered as we reached the bottom.

"Why do the adults still defend the nest, even with their chicks gone?" I wondered aloud, running my hand over my hair. I realized that we'd underestimated the ferocity of a parent eagle; I had come very close to having my head opened.

"I hope the others have more luck this year," Anne sighed.

We were sure that there were one or two other nests on the island—eagles were a common sight. Often we counted almost a dozen, riding the thermals on the summit. Some flew in pairs and some were immatures, tawny and mottled, without the crisp white head and tail they would bear as five-year-old adults. During the day they picked at carcasses washed up by the tide. At dusk they perched, hunched and still as gargoyles, on the edges of the colonies, waiting for birds returning from sea. Like the coastal salmon rivers, to which the eagles would migrate in the fall, Triangle Island provided a dependable concentration of food. In other habitats each pair could require a large territory; here pairs could live side by side.

As we began our walk back from the nest, I glanced back at the two eagles, watching us from their perches. Ornithology described bird behaviour in terms of predictable responses to specific stimuli: the light of the seasons, the flash of prey, the calls and postures of territoriality and mating, the begging of young, the threat of a predator near their nest. Was there an avian form of grief? How long would it be before the eagles abandoned their empty cradle and returned to their solitary lives?

June 10

The island finally awakened from winter. The lady ferns lining the paths were armpit-high. Above the beach we found small golden flowers pressed close to the sand. We kneeled to check for the fine silver hairs under the leaves, which identified them as

Part One

silverweed. Where fresh water found its way through rock, yellow monkey flower glittered.

Pausing for a view of Vancouver Island on our way up to the trail, we heard the sound of buzzing flight. A small dark bird, slightly larger than a bumblebee, dropped out of the sky, vibrated near Anne's shoulder, inspected her red sweater, then stopped at a nearby columbine.

We sat down and watched the male rufous hummingbird.

"It's amazing he can survive out here," I said, as we watched him hovering on blurred wings, his scarlet neck gorgets flashing in the sun.

Searching for nectar, he probed gently, his curved beak exactly fitting the curve of the flower spurs. Weighing less than a nickel, he seemed a flamboyant experiment, conjured for the pure joy of miniature novelty and beauty.

"The teachers at my Catholic schools would say that's proof of God's existence."

"How is that?" I asked.

"That the way everything is perfectly suited to its life, could only be planned."

Silverweed

silver hairs & under leaves

Potentilla anserina
edible roots were cooked
by men at Kwakiutl feasts.

Part One

tiny yellow spots on petals

a little saxifrage - flowering among the rocks - probably Saxifraga ferruginea

"What did they say about Darwin?" I asked.

Anne smiled wryly. "I didn't learn about evolution until I got to university."

Shifting in the long grass, I reached out and turned a nodding columbine flower upwards, gazing into the rosy light of its throat, recalling the naturalist Loren Eiseley's description of the emergence of flowering plants, just before the dinosaurs disappeared, as a "soundless, violent explosion" that lasted millions of years.

The hummingbird suddenly flew straight up into the air. Stopping abruptly, as if he had run into an invisible ceiling, he hovered for a moment then dropped like a stone, with a rapid, staccato sound created by the vibration of stiff tail feathers. Just before he drove his body beak first into the ground, he pulled up with a flourish, hovered above us and flew off. I recognized this extravagant performance as the J-flight, a mating display. Was there a female nearby? Had two rufous hummingbirds, by some miracle, made it here? That he had made an ocean crossing that had thwarted the hardiest of mariners seemed incredible. Yet this was only the last stop on a long journey from his lush Mexican wintering grounds.

How had the first exhausted hummingbird stumbled upon this small oasis? Triangle had not always teemed with life. Glaciers had only released the land from perpetual winter about 10,000 years ago.

Not long ago this land was a slate wiped clean by ice. Life had to find it.

Like the birds that had colonized Triangle Island, most new inhabitants had arrived by air. Winds delivered the very lightest of seeds or spores of lichens, mosses, ferns, and fungi as well as spiders riding strands of silk, and other insects like flies, bees, wasps, beetles, dragonflies...and birds. With the birds came the seeds, carried on feet or feathers, or in digestive tracts, that would sow more new life.

I looked down at the meadows below me. In the last two weeks they had burst into flower with chocolate lilies and pink montia, saxifrage and buttercups. Giant stalks of cow parsnip bore platter-sized flower heads crowded with beetles, like waiters offering hors d'oeuvres to the song sparrows who landed on them to stuff their beaks. Orange-crowned warblers flew up from salmonberry thickets like bright lures cast into the lake of sky.

The plants that grew on these slopes, as well as on the beaches and high plateaus of the island were all familiar—they were the ones I knew from hiking and camping trips on the west coast of Vancouver Island. I followed the scattered line of the Scott Islands back to its dark blue silhouette. These islands might have puzzled even Darwin.

He had turned his curious gaze on not only the inhabitants of islands but islands themselves and observed two kinds: oceanic and continental. The first were made of lava or coral and had no mammals or amphibians (because they had no way of getting there). The second were islands clustered near continental shores.

They were made of all kinds of rocks; their inhabitants, including mammals and amphibians were a legacy of the continent they had once been part of, like descendants of a marooned ship.

Though never a part of North America, the Scott Islands look like continental islands. Time had washed them up onto this shelf, within easy reach of nearby life. Familiar plants, insects, and songbirds had found their way to Triangle from the continent, leap-frogging islands along the way.

Darwin knew that on remote islands, like the Galapagos, species can change rapidly, even evolve into many forms—the "adaptive radiation" he described in the famous finches.

I watched the hummingbird stop at the next spray of columbine flowers, bright as blood among the pale grass. Except for the hum of his wings, the waves and wind, the island was quiet. As always it felt a world apart, frozen in time. It was, I reminded myself, neither. Even here, in the short time since life got a foothold, evolution had already been at work on it. Invisibly tucked among the grasses and shrubs were the island's only small mammals, white-footed mice and meadow voles. They may have arrived clinging to soil or branches on tangled rafts of spruce and cedar wrenched by floods from forests, or later, hidden among the cargo of Native canoes.

They are distinctly different from those of the continent. Many of the mice have a white blaze on their foreheads. Probably Triangle Island was colonized by a tiny group of mice, some of which bore the blaze. Eventually it became common. But the most dramatic difference is that island mice and voles are bigger than their mainland cousins.

As I got up and brushed the grass seeds off my knees, I scanned the island below. From this distance, the meeting of land and sea looked tidier, less ambiguous than it really was.

June 18

Within each nest lay a plump egg. While the puffins quietly incubated we finally had time to explore. We had been here many weeks, but there were still places we had not seen. Sometimes, though the island was only a little over a mile long and 355 acres

Chocolate Lily

Fritillaria camschatcensis

A foul smelling flowers attract fly pollinators

other name: Rice Root refers to starchy bulbs which were important food to coastal peoples

Part One

RED COLUMBINE

← nectar glands in spurs

Aquilegia formosa

in area, it seemed as big as a kingdom. Parts of it were a day's arduous travel. Other than its beaches, most of its land was poised on the top of a fortress of cliffs. Its curving shoreline of about three miles was interrupted by sheer walls of stone, passable only at low tide.

We set out, lingering for once as we walked the beach, jumping from log to log. Ancient giants, bleached white as bone—Douglas fir, Sitka spruce, red and yellow cedar from the great coastal forest to the east—had been tossed high on the beach by years of winter storms.

There were some exotic woods here too. Mahogany and teak, their dark heartwood hidden under a white patina, were swept in by winds and currents raking across the Pacific from the Orient.

The currents left other reminders of their origins. The shore was littered with debris. We dug among tangles of polypropylene rope anchored deep in sand, to pull out bottles of hair tonic, dish detergent, and cooking oil, all covered in indecipherable Japanese characters. Prodded by wind, this litter probably took five years to float across the north Pacific to Triangle's shores.

What Anne and I were really searching for among the driftwood were glass balls, the kind once used as floats by Japanese fishing fleets. Though they were replaced by plastic years ago, glass balls, broken away from nets, continued to swirl in the great circling Pacific currents. They still wash up on the West Coast. Most of them are smashed on rocky shores, but on sandy beaches or riding high water they can come to their final rest a perfect pale blue-green sphere, like crystallized seawater itself, blown hollow.

With the approaching solstice the tides had swung low. The sea rolled back, exposing its soft underbelly. We walked the wrack line, sliding over great corrugated straps of Laminaria kelp lying in ropy heaps.

On an exposed headland usually scoured with waves "California" mussels as long as my hand and heavy as stones, clustered thickly on the reef. Evidence of the brutal surf was everywhere. Any living thing that survived here was adapted to hold on tight under deluges that would be tidal waves to us. Purple starfish, their resistant flesh embedded with a stucco of calcium, clung with hundreds of tube feet to the rocks. Nearby a tiny mossy chiton, its umber back covered in a chain mail of linked plates, gripped a crack. A small forest of stocky seaweed, flexible stalks cemented to the shore, whipped back and forth in the surf, shaking their fronds.

In the slanting light of late afternoon we picked our way through the tide line. Under dank overhangs we found colonial animals called tunicates, which formed gelatinous quilts of cream, pink, plum and scarlet. Splashed among them were brilliant orange patches of sponge and cup coral. A slimy, obscene-looking sac, which hung dripping into the pool below, recoiled from my touch. Constellations of sea stars—leather stars, bat stars, vermilion stars and sun stars glistened against wet rock. Many more jammed themselves tightly into dark clefts.

This was a dangerous day. Only on the few extreme tides of summer is the low intertidal laid bare to drying winds and burning sun. Some animals would not survive the exposure, others would become prey for feasting crows, gulls and eagles.

Part One

We stretched out on our stomachs, gazing into a deep tide pool. Sea anemones waved like green silk scarves, in the pulse of the dropping tide. I lowered my hand into the soft centre to feel the tentacles close around it, slightly rough, like a cat's tongue. As a child, I loved this strange sensation that I was communicating with the vegetable world; only later did I learn that they were animals, related to jellyfish. The stinging cells (or nematocysts) on the tentacles, which tugged on my fingers, were toxic enough to stun small swimming prey.

Startled by my shifting shadow, hermit crabs retreated into their empty snail shells. Backing up the right-twisting corridors of their adopted homes they dragged their huge right claws in last, as if pulling over-sized couches through narrow doors. Stone-coloured sculpins—small, darting tide pool fishes with fan-like fins—withdrew beneath brittle branches of pink coralline algae.

The bottom of the pool was tiled with urchins: green, scarlet and purple. The green urchins were small, about the size of a mandarin orange, but they made up for this with one of the longest scientific names: *Strongylocentrotis drobachiensis*. Lying near the pool was a hollow white sphere, bumped and pitted like Braille—the empty calcareous shell or "test" of a sea urchin. The spines were shed long ago, revealing swirling rows of perforations, holes through which soft inner parts of the animal reached out into the world: tiny stalked jaws for keeping its surface clean, filamentous tube feet for shifting position and moving food to the mouth. On the underside of the test was a delicate basket of hinged plates. I dried my hands on my jeans and dug my old copy of Ed Ricketts' *Between Pacific Tides* out of my pack.

Ricketts identified the strange structure in my hands as an "Aristotle's lantern." It supported a rosette of five tiny white teeth with which the urchin "cuts seaweed into portions small enough for ingestion in the huge, coiled intestine." Ricketts praised the gonads of urchins as a delicacy: *"We have sampled these gonads, eaten à l'Italienne (raw) with French bread, and found them very good..."*

"Anne, Ricketts says sea urchin gonads are better than caviar," I proclaimed.

I rolled up my sleeve, leaned over the edge, plunged my arm

lowest tides of summer uncovered walls of sea stars, anemones, tunicates & sponges

into the frigid water and pulled out a scarlet urchin. It was the size of a small melon, with spines as long as fingers rotating on their little ball-and-socket joints, motioning me silently. Despite its forbidding appearance the shell was broken easily with a rock. The animal inside resembled an exotic fruit, freshly peeled, with five bright yellow segments of stippled egg sacs radiating from top to bottom. I plunged my fingers into the slippery mass and peeled one back, letting it rest in my palm. I raised it to my mouth and swallowed the cool, salty stuff quickly. It left a faint iodine aftertaste like the distilled essence of the sea.

I licked my fingertips and passed the urchin to Anne, who ate some with a thoughtful look, contemplating the odd taste.

"Too bad we don't have French bread," she sighed.

As we walked farther, stopping to look into pool after pool, I imagined the excitement Ricketts would have felt on the pristine shores of Triangle. He had been a friend of John Steinbeck's and the model for the biologist "Doc" in *Cannery Row*. The two men were just about to leave for a collecting trip along this coast when Ricketts was killed in his car at a rail crossing in 1948.

At my feet, the cold water hummed with compressed life engaged in the business of keeping tiny metabolic fires burning. Sedentary worms filtered plankton with tufts of red "feather-duster" feeding tentacles blooming from the ends of their leathery tubes. Thousands of barnacles honeycombed the rock, opening their hinged plates and beating the water with minute, jointed digits to capture tiny prey. Carnivorous snails drilled through mussel shells. Predatory sponges bored slowly with acid into the shells of purple-hinged rock scallops. The pool was a hive of stinging cells, mined with the mouths of sculpins open and lying in wait for the next meal.

Hours later, as the tide crept back, we picked our way home along the beach. The kelp, anchored by gnarled "holdfasts" to the bottom, rose on slender stipes and arranged its fronds on the surface of the water again, like the long hair of mermaids. I heard Anne cry out and turned quickly, afraid that she had caught an ankle in the shifting logs. Smiling widely, she held up a globe the size of a grapefruit—a glass ball, gleaming in the evening light.

Part One

June 22

The midsummer light lingered; long after sunset the cobalt sky was luminous. In order to gather the last of our krill samples we had to stay up past midnight for darkness to fall on the Cassin's auklet colonies. By the time we finished it was two in the morning.

We walked home, not speaking, listening to the waves break on the beach just beyond our circle of light. A gibbous moon rose above Puffin Rock. I turned off my headlamp. The air was lucid, uncontaminated by city light, and I could see clearly the familiar patterns of shadow on the moon shaped by imagination: crabs, rabbits, donkeys, the old man staring from the pale coin face that always lands heads up in the night sky.

I looked through my binoculars. The moon's cold mountain ranges cast hard shadows. The whimsical shapes resolved instantly into parched lowlands, pockmarked with the craters of meteors and volcanoes—the "seas" first seen clearly by Galileo.

I was close to the water's edge. The moon, recently full near the solstice, had brought the tides clambering high up the beach, almost flooding the oystercatchers' nest. The white frill of shore break seemed to cast its own light. I walked towards it.

At my feet the waves shattered into flying sparks. I threw a rock and it seared through the water like a shooting star. The sea was ablaze with the cold fire of bioluminescence. The summer light had ignited huge plankton blooms, probably of the organism known as Noctiluca (literally, "night light"). When disturbed or moved, a chemical reaction within them releases light. Each pulse of light is only one tenth of a second. Millions of individuals firing are liquid light—pouring around anything that moves through it. In other waters I had swum in this light, caught it in my eyelashes, cloaked my limbs with it. But this sea was too cold, this night too late, and I too tired. I turned on my headlamp and followed Anne down the beach.

June 25

We had not had fresh fish since the halibut season. I rummaged through the kindling for a short piece of driftwood, tied a fish hook and line to it, and poked my head in the door where

Blood Star

← smooth skin

Henricia leviuscula — females brood their eggs.

Part One

"Fluffy Sculpin" stranded in a tiny tidepool

Anne was sitting on her bunk carefully cutting patches from a piece of oil-stained canvas we had found on the beach.

She would stay and finish the job of stitching them to the torn knees of her jeans.

I was glad to go by myself. Our work and isolation narrowed life into practical, repetitive routines. Lately I felt as though parts of me were disappearing. I needed time alone to recover them, to let my thoughts wander.

I headed for where the east point of the beach dissolved into reefs. On this shore, water rushed into surge channels, rising to dark walls at high tide. If I walked there on a low tide, I had to be careful to turn back before I was caught behind the sea's moat.

The water was beginning to fall as I set out. The rock was angular, slick with weed below the tide line and blackened with a fine layer of encrusting lichen in the splash zone where it was moistened with salt spray.

I concentrated on finding my route and slipped into a trance-like state—until I rounded a corner and was startled by a snort. A male sea lion the size of a compact car reared up slowly, six feet in front of me. As I backed away, the flesh rippled beneath his tawny fur. Not knowing whether he was preparing to charge or retreat, and not wanting to find out, I scrambled back around the corner. Though he looked ungainly, I knew from watching sea lions spar that he could move very fast when he wanted. Unlike seals, which must wriggle their overstuffed-sausage bodies on land, sea lions have agile flippers, front and back. The seals of the circus, balancing balls on their noses, are actually California sea lions, prized for their playful natures. This was a Steller's or northern sea lion. They are bigger than Californias (the males can weigh a ton) and appear to have no sense of humour—especially at this time of year, when they are deadly serious about breeding.

Triangle Island is one of British Columbia's biggest sea lion colonies. In late spring up to eight hundred animals arrive. Looking down on them from the island's heights, a researcher once observed that their teeming rookeries looked like pieces of meat crawling with maggots. The offshore islets where they congregate are noisy and stained with blood and feces. At this time of year females give birth and males compete with each other for harems, charging, and sometimes goring each other with their sharp, dog-like teeth. Many bulls sport scars and festering wounds. Night and day we heard the males belching and roaring; the rookeries' fishy smell of decay swirled around the island.

Driven from the point, I struck off along the spine of a reef until I found an overhang and deep water. I dropped my hook, baited with cheese. The sky was marbled with cloud, the sea smooth and pale as abalone. I jigged the line idly. Its filament pierced the water delicately, a translucent stitch between two realms. To the people of this coast, the world above the sea and the world below the sea were mirror images of each other—complex hierarchies of men and creatures where natural and supernatural coexisted. The underwater world was reached by canoe, through a cave where the tides rushed in and out. Piled high on either side of this channel were the bones of the drowned. Only after passing the places to which all the driftwood, toilet sticks, coal and feathers went did the traveller reach the house of Sea Lion.

Part One

This house, a mountain far out in the ocean, was painted with sea lions, the ends of the magnificent beams carved with them.

Did the seafaring Kwakiutl somehow know about the seamounts rising almost to the surface, far offshore? A puff of exhalation drew me from my thoughts. The nose and forehead of a sea lion broke the surface near the point, nostrils widening for breath before he dove, back arching in a shining curve. Underwater, sea lions are transformed. Their heavy, awkward bodies become agile, twisting and turning in a ballet of grace and speed.

I reflected that these waters were not always such an idyllic haven for sea lions. Fishermen were encouraged to shoot any near their nets. Even the federal Department of Fisheries, believing that sea lions were salmon predators, made annual trips to rookeries and haul-outs from 1912 to 1968 to kill them. The first provincial biological survey of the island, in the early fifties, coincided with one of these expeditions: "rifle and machine-gun fire dispersed the population, with some 2,000 animals reported killed. When the smoke had cleared away, there appeared to be many more live sea-lions in the area than dead ones, which seems to indicate that originally the population had been very large."

These animals were not protected until 1970, with the International Treaty on Marine Mammals. Recent research on their diet has since shown that during the non-breeding season they do eat schooling fishes like herring, hake, pollock, dogfish and salmon, though salmon makes up a small percentage of their diet. During the breeding season they eat reef fish. The sea lions and I were fishing for the same dinner.

I hoped they were having more luck than I was. As I began to pull up my hook I felt a small tug and jerked the line, willing the hook to catch. A shudder ran up the line as I gathered it in, wrapping it on my driftwood reel. A dusky head with a large gaping mouth split the skin of water—a black rockfish. It wasn't big, but it was fresh! I pulled it up onto the rock and whacked it frantically with my stick. Its black eye, rimmed with copper stared up at me, still and opaque.

I hurried home, giving the lounging sea lion a wide berth, being careful not to get between it and the sea. I showed Anne my

a lone male Steller's sea lion

catch then carried it to the shore to fillet it, running the knife down the spine on either side of the dorsal fin, careful of the heavy, sharp spines that could inflict painful stab wounds that fester for days. By the time I had cut away the bones and removed the large head, there was barely enough for two cats. But we were overjoyed at the prospect of meat. It was not until we returned home and began heating the frying pan that I noticed the flesh was dimpled with tiny coiled worms—parasites.

Our hearts were set on my hard won dinner. Grimacing, we cut the worms, one by one, out of the flesh, and threw the meagre remains into the pan.

July 2

I sat bolt upright, shaking my hair and cursing. For a few minutes there was silence. Then, one by one, they emerged from the dark, running onto my sleeping bag, over my head, in a mad dash for the kitchen, to gnaw on the food cupboard.

Where did the term "quiet as a mouse" come from? In the last weeks the mouse population had exploded—all night long, mice chewed on the floorboards and through the walls. We put out traps, but they made little difference. Like a teeming army, there were always fresh recruits. To make matters worse, like almost every one of the isolated islands anchored on the continental shelf, Triangle had evolved a race of giant mice. These were somewhere between the size of normal mice and rats. If I placed one in my hand, its body was longer than my palm, and the tail hung several inches past the tips of my fingers.

I lay in the dark pondering why jumbo-sized mice are selected on islands. Apparently, bigger mice had bigger young with a better chance of survival. Researchers, finding that molars of Triangle Island's largest mice were almost worn away, concluded that island mice were older than most mainland mice. They had fewer predators on isolated islands. Pity, I thought, as I pulled my covers up around my chin.

A crinkly, papery sound reminded me that I had left a package of crackers out and I hissed softly under my breath. As I climbed out of bed silence immediately fell. I padded to the next room, where I locked the food in the cupboard, then settled again under

Part One

my blankets still thinking about what I had read of island gigantism. At least a few animals were putting on weight in our kitchen but I wondered if Triangle's mice were still evolving into a larger form. I knew that evolution is not always the slow and steady process we imagine, especially on islands. Mice collected in the early part of the century on an island off the southern tip of the Queen Charlotte Islands had relatively smaller tails than mainland mice. Shortly after the first collections, rats were introduced to the island. By the 1960s mice collected there had longer tails. It appears that to survive the rats' predation and competition for food, more agile mice with longer tails evolved very quickly.

As I closed my eyes, trying to go to sleep before the mice emerged again, I thanked God that rats had not made it to Triangle Island. If they had, there was a good chance I would not be here. Once rats arrive on a seabird colony, it is only a matter of time before birds vanish. Ground-nesting seabirds have no defence against these voracious predators. On the little Scottish island of Ailsa Craig, rats landed accidentally after a shipwreck in 1889. By 1947 the population of 250,000 common puffins was reduced to thirty birds. Many seabird colonies worldwide have suffered the same fate, sometimes from the introduction of other animals like raccoons, cats, dogs or weasels. In the 1930s mink and raccoon were introduced for their fur to Lanz and Cox, the Scott Islands closest to Vancouver Island. Trap lines were abandoned in the 1960s, leaving the islands with resident predators, which most likely decimated auklets nesting there.

Anyone who comes to work on Triangle Island must follow "rat protocol." The instructions refer to the possible introduction of rats on the island as "arguably nothing less than the worst ecological disaster in British Columbia history." It goes on to say:

> All gear and supplies destined for Triangle will be transported in boxes completely sealed with tape at the time of packing. The boxes must be known to not contain a rat before they are sealed, and they must be sealed in such a way that if a rat has entered the box, its entry will be obvious from a hole chewed in it. The boxes are to be inspected before taking them to the island. Any boxes with open tears or signs of entry must be immediately emptied, repacked and resealed.

Part One

> If the boxes come by ship, they must be inspected again before they are brought ashore, in case rats in the hold infest them.

It was incredible that there were no rats on Triangle Island after years of lightkeepers in the early part of the century, and recent years of summer research. Where humans are, rats are never far behind. If they did arrive it would be impossible to get rid of them.

I pulled my sleeping bag over my head. Compared to rats, the giant mice of Triangle Island, scratching and gnawing at my dreams, were a small irritation. I tried to think of them as many coastal people did, as helpful creatures, tiny mouse-women, who appeared when someone needed a guide, an aid or a messenger. But the only thing I needed was to fall asleep. When I finally did, first light was bleaching the stars from the sky. The mice retreated, vanishing completely until the next nightfall.

July 11

I stood on the shore, corpses washing up at my feet. More bodies were strewn along the beach, their faces bloodless and unfamiliar. There had been an accident at sea, but I couldn't fathom what to do next. The bodies were too heavy to pull out of the water. Finally, I ran up to the trailer and tried to call for help on the radio. I could hear the call ringing, ringing. Nobody answered. Why wouldn't anybody answer?

I reached over to turn off my alarm, dragged from dream, and checked the time: 4:30 a.m.

In the kitchen, I poured instant milk over cold cereal and inspected the traps. I carried the night's catch—three grey bodies with pale pink on the soles of their feet and the inside of their soft ears—by their supple tails, to the back door. Outside it was black and raining hard. I wanted nothing more than to climb back into the warm lair of my sleeping bag. I was sick of mice and rain, sick of this godforsaken island, its mute stone, the endless monologue of waves. In the end, the birds would survive, or not, with or without me.

I stood for a moment listening to the rain on the roof, packed my knapsack, pulled on my rain gear, and stretched the strap of my headlamp over my sou'wester. With a sigh I stepped out into the dark.

Climbing the steep trail I concentrated on hand and footholds, aware only of the world within the circle of my light. When I got to the top I folded myself into the tiny plywood blind which had miraculously survived May's gale, and took out a notebook and tape recorder. I watched the drops sliding past my face, off the peak of the blind. Shifting my cramped limbs, I turned my tape recorder on, sang a few lines of a Joni Mitchell song and played it back—a thin voice in an amphitheatre of wind. I erased it, turned the tape recorder off and waited.

The rain stopped. The crescent moon, its round, dark burden faintly lit—the "old moon in the new moon's arms"—hung above the horizon. A smudge appeared in the east, growing brighter until the sky over Vancouver Island looked like orange lamp glass, streaked with milky clouds. A bird flew toward me from the direction of the sea. Dangling from the prow of its bill were the heads and tails of silver fish.

In the last week Anne and I had found many of the puffin eggs hatching. First the egg developed fine cracks, then a pale tip of tiny beak appeared. We heard the chick peeping as it excavated its way out of the egg with its "egg tooth," a small hard point that eventually drops off.

The chicks emerge wet and exhausted, but quickly dry into tiny balls of slate-coloured down. They are not helpless for the first weeks of life like robin or sparrow nestlings; right away they begin teetering around on their big feet and unsteady legs. Photophobia keeps them from wandering out of their burrows. If they are removed from the nest, they quickly head for the nearest dark place.

Even with luxuriant down coats the newly hatched chicks cannot keep themselves warm enough; for about a week, parents share brooding. At the same time they begin the gruelling schedule of food delivery they must sustain for the next six or seven weeks, if the chick is going to be strong enough to fledge.

I may have been up early, but the bird with the beakful of fish had already put in several hours of work and miles of flying. Trying to be as still as I could, I watched it bank and land in front

Part One

of a marked burrow about twenty feet away from me. I had weighed the egg there just a few days ago. The puffin stood in the rosy morning light. It shook its golden tufts, still wet from diving, and gave me a quick glance. The birds had become used to the new blind on the colony, but this one, on its first feeding trips of the season, was wary. As if to remind him that his age-old adversary was still his greatest, a peregrine streaked overhead and the puffin ducked into his burrow. The falcon flew soundlessly over the colony, alert, ready to veer with lightning speed after unwary prey. I could just make out the helmet of feathers that covered his head and nape and ran in a wedge below his eyes. His whitish breast was heavily spotted and his back and tail were dark like his head. He was a Peale's peregrine, typical of the coast, duskier than a mainland bird, as if tinted by the rock and dense forest. This bird also had young to feed. Just a few weeks old, three or four down-covered young huddled in a nearby aerie, an overhung ledge high on a cliff. They would be waiting for their breakfast: a plump puffin, or a Cassin's or rhinoceros auklet who left the colony too late and got caught travelling without cover of darkness. Though I was relieved my puffin had been quick to duck, I wished I could see the notorious "peregrine stoop," which has been reported to occur at speeds of over 185 miles per hour. It was once thought that peregrines strike with their feet clenched in a fist, but high-speed film shows they strike from above with all four toes fully extended. An explosion of feathers follows the impact, and the victim falls. The peregrine may dive again and pick it out of the air, or follow it to the ground.

There was probably more than one pair of peregrines on the island. Like eagles, they could share a small territory because there was plenty of food. But peregrines are much more dependent on seabirds than the omnivorous, adaptable eagles. Almost every peregrine aerie on the coast is within a few miles of a seabird colony.

The puffin emerged from its burrow a few moments later. The danger had passed. It shook itself again and flew back to sea. I reached for the tape recorder and entered the time of feeding, an estimate of the number of fish, and the burrow number.

By the time my shift was over, the sun was high. I shook the rain off my slicker, stuffed it into my pack and climbed down,

Part One

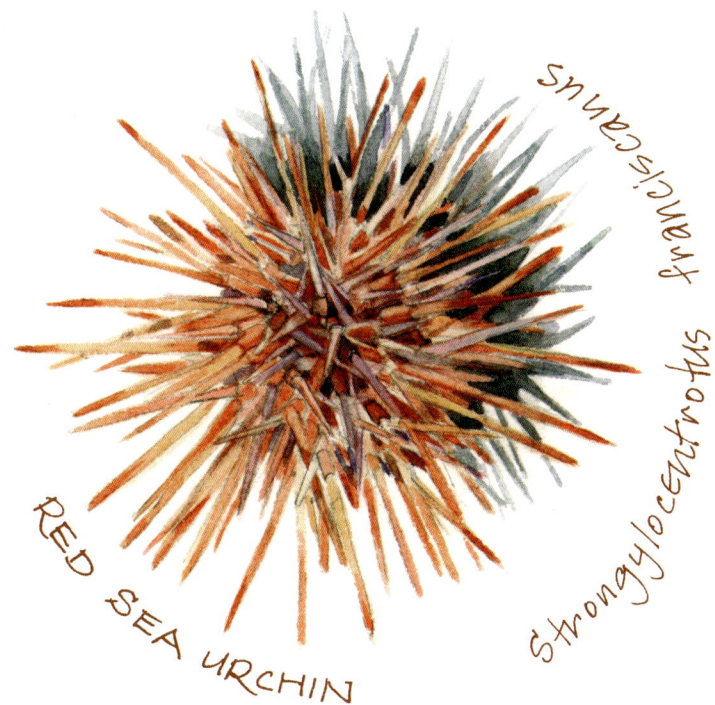

RED SEA URCHIN
Strongylocentrotus franciscanus

picking my way between pools strung like pearls along strands of reef. Lush, trailing feather boa seaweed undulated in the pulse of the tide. As I knelt to poke around in it, hoping to find kelp crabs, blood stars and chitons, I noticed a dark shape, a small lifeless bundle bumping and rolling gently back and forth at the edge of the pool. I pulled the weeds back from it. The creature was covered in chocolate fur. It had a soft muzzle, stiff whiskers and sharp canines. It was a Steller's sea lion, just a few days old. Except for the tiny flippers it looked like a drowned puppy. Sea lions, like seals evolved from land mammals. They have still not mastered the art of mating and giving birth at sea. I could hear the dull roar, rising from the chaotic colony, on the rocky island just around the corner. This pup was probably crushed by an adult sea lion—a charging male or panicking female. I laid the seaweed back down and walked on. Even in the season of birth, death was always close by.

115

July 13

    I walked the same route on the shore each day: down the path from our trailer to the logs thrown high on the beach. I jumped to the big old yellow cedar, stepped down from it to a Sitka spruce sanded smooth by weather, and walked its length until it buried itself in the beach. Picking my way through the cobblestones I eventually came to blocks of dark rock with ledges I could climb like stairs and deep diagonal fissures to leap over. Past these rocks the trail met the grass again at the base of the pinnacle where the eagle nest perched, on the western end of the beach. Then I crossed "The Gap" between the main island and Puffin Rock. When the tide was high this route was covered. If we forgot to check the chart we had to wade in chest-deep, freezing water, holding our packs high above our heads. Or we had to sit on the rocks below Puffin Rock and wait for the tide to drop before we could go home.

    Today the tide was low. Oystercatchers picked their way along the shore, prodding and turning the gleaming weeds. The nest we'd discovered in May was empty. We had not noticed the eggs hatching on their hard bed of beach stones. Emerging into the glare of the sky and keen-eyed predators, the chicks abandoned their nest quickly. Unlike the blind newborn sparrow chicks huddled in nests hidden in shrubs, oystercatchers hatch all legs and feet, ready to run.

    From three eggs, two speckled chicks had survived and now scurried after a parent. The adult, up to its pink ankles in water, stopped and cocked its head slightly, focusing one yellow eye on the tide, the other at the sky. It jabbed at something near its right foot. Lifting its head as a chick rushed over, it passed a glistening morsel of shore crab from one set of red enamel chopsticks to another.

    This chick would shadow its parent for months, learning the tricks of the oystercatcher trade: how to sneak up on an oyster or clam and plunge its bill between the shells, severing the muscles that hold them together, how to loosen mussels from their mooring and shatter them with short powerful blows, and how to pry up a limpet or chiton or quickly spear a sea worm.

    Once, birds were magical. The oystercatcher's furtive existence,

Part One

at the boundary of water and land—and its arresting colour scheme of deep black with yellow eyes and crimson beak—made it mysterious. First to give alarm and fly from danger, it was like the Native shaman, a guardian of the people.

As I drew near, the oystercatchers, engrossed in the pleasures of low tide, finally noticed me. They crouched nervously, and flew off, whistling like bosuns, over the territory we shared, the only habitable space the island made for us—a narrow edge, backed up against cliffs by miles of ocean.

July 15

A strangely seductive fog descended on the island. Shut in this white room I no longer felt dwarfed by towering cliffs, wide sea and endless sky stretching out around me. When I collected firewood from the beach in the morning, I could see only as far as the shore. I returned misted like a greenhouse plant, droplets clinging to my hair and eyelashes and soaking into the shoulders of my sweater.

Anne and I spent the afternoon inside tending the fire. Rolling the threadbare cuffs of a blue work shirt up past her forearms, she punched down bread dough with her small strong hands, stuffed the dough into a greased coffee tin, and balanced it on the stove top. Then she sat down and bent over pages of data—burrow slope and length, egg and chick weights—written in a short-stemmed, compact script. Her hair had grown out since its ragged cut. It was a cap of sun-bleached curls. Every few minutes she looked up and carefully turned the tin.

"What do you want to listen to?"

Anne gave a distracted shrug. "You choose."

J.J. Cale sang "Magnolia." The familiar loneliness rose and I pushed it back in the familiar way, by keeping busy.

On the table below the window I set out a dissecting kit with scalpel and tweezers, needle and thread, and a bag of cotton wool. I had found a rhinoceros auklet on the beach that morning and I was determined to stuff it.

I laid the dead bird beside the instruments. Its eyes were cloudy under half-closed, dry lids. At the inner corner of each eye was a small triangle of pale membrane, the "third eyelid" or nictitans.

Fireweed

This is the lid that blinks the bird's eye, moving quickly over it from inner to outer edge. In auklets, the membrane has a clear lens-shaped window that lies over the eye, like a contact lens, when the bird dives.

Barrel-chested and slightly larger than a pigeon, rhinoceros auklets are puffins' plain cousins. They have wispy white cheek plumes and a small pale orange beak with a homely, horn-like projection at the base. They are burrow nesters, like puffins, but they only arrive on the colonies at dusk.

While the puffins' wheeling flights had broken down into a pandemonium of individually circling birds, the rhinoceros auklets seemed to perfect their synchronous display as summer advanced. There was a large colony on the slopes behind our trailer. Each night more birds circled, a dark whirlpool in the night sky over the bay. Most of the flights were clockwise, but sometimes a bird flew in a suicidal counter-current, collided with another, and fell stunned to the beach.

I looked carefully at my bird. It showed no signs of injury. Other than its vacant eye, it was perfect. Perhaps its neck was broken by just such a collision. I picked up the tweezers and took a deep breath. I had stuffed a bird once before—a saw-whet owl, which I dug out of a biology department freezer, where birds that had been run over by cars or flown into plate glass windows were stored for the ornithology classes. I had never had a chance to look so closely at an owl and yet, the task of preparing its skin held none of the pleasure of a fleeting glimpse in a dark forest.

Not that long ago any biologist worth his salt would be an expert taxidermist. Even thirty years ago, biologists carried guns and nets and left the island with boxes of plants, birds, marine life and insects. They were added to the provincial museum's research collections from all over the province.

I picked out the rhinoceros auklet's eyes with the tweezers, then took a slender instrument with a blunt end and began to break up the brains. As I pulled the liverish mash out of the sockets, I recalled my ornithology professor, a thin man with a heron-like crest of silver hair, enthusiastically stating "birds are eye-brained, in the way fish are nose-brained." Their optic lobes are large, like ours. But their cerebellums, the part responsible for co-ordination and balance, are much bigger. Flight demands

Part One

precise orientation in space. The bird I held in my hands was also able to move deftly underwater. I swabbed the delicate skull, and stuffed it with cotton, until it spilled out the eyes in a blank, white stare. Then I picked up the scalpel, parted the feathers below the ribs, and gently cut into soft, wine-coloured skin to remove body organs.

The smell of baking bread mingled with the ferrous smell of the bird as I stuffed and carefully sewed it up. I tied a tag to the leathery black twig of leg, then stepped back to examine my handiwork. It looked like it had been dragged in by a cat. I was inexperienced at handling the dead. It showed in my work: if the skin contours of a stuffed bird are not just right, the feathers do not lie flat.

Just hours earlier, the auklet had preened its feathers into weightless, waterproof armour, and had dived into green light. Its belly had been full of tiny bones and silver scales. Perhaps, I thought sadly, it had a chick in a burrow, and a mate fishing. It was a specimen now: "Rhinoceros auklet, *Cerorhinca monocerata*, Triangle Island, July 10, 1980." At the end of the summer I would take it to the provincial museum in Victoria, where it would be placed, breast up, wings folded, among a line of rhinoceros auklets in a wide drawer.

In the evening a pale blue flag of sky flew behind the parting haze, and the rocky rim of the bay emerged slowly. By morning, the island had disappeared again.

After three days of fog my mind went fuzzy. The fusion of sea, sky and land blurred other boundaries, up and down, close and far, real and imaginary. I developed a deep longing for maps. I wanted to linger over the details of places I knew, and to imagine places I had never been, to trace the course of the Ganges, the spine of the Andes. The swarming print would remind me that there were landscapes not deserted, but worn with living.

Every so often we heard a motor in the distance, a passing freighter or fish boat. But it always faded, leaving us cut off from the world, timeless, dimensionless. No one could reach us; no pilot would fly in this weather and no boat would land unless equipped with radar and a captain capable of picking his way through Triangle's rocks. Our radio worked so rarely that we seldom tried to call out.

Triangle Island's affinity for fog was one of the reasons the lighthouse was eventually abandoned. A simple foghorn at sea level could have warned mariners off her perilous shores but it would have been impossible for the staff, living 600 feet up, to maintain. Mariners were drawn into the folds of fog. Triangle's light was not only ineffective, it was a hazard.

But fog was not only a spectre during the winter on Triangle Island. The weather records show that in 1911 the summit was shrouded in fog for 240 days. Even in summer Triangle's mammoth light was obscured as warm, moist sea air met the cool air at the edge of the continent, created by upwellings.

Today, the weather report on our scratchy transistor said fog lay in strands along the outer coast from Vancouver Island to California. For miles the sky was blue, swept clean by the blithe Pacific high. Below it, a grey carpet unrolled from the sea.

The Tlingit, the seafaring people of Alaska, believed a seabird, the petrel, created fog, releasing it from under his hat. Petrels are sparrow-like seabirds, small enough to hold in your hand, light as sea foam. A few hundred nested in burrows on Triangle Island. I had never seen them, as they came and went in the dark, but sometimes I caught a whiff of their peculiar musky smell. The name "petrel" is in honour of St. Peter. At Jesus' bidding, Peter walked on water, but "when he saw the wind was boisterous, he was afraid…" Losing faith, Peter began to sink. In calm waters petrels dip and dance on the surface, feeding. But in rough seas, like St. Peter, they sink and hover in the troughs of waves. To European mariners, petrels were "Mother Carey's chickens." Their sudden appearance was a warning that severe storms were on the way.

July 19

I lay on my side, and stretched my arm deep into the earth, feeling blindly for the warm ball of a newly hatched chick. My fingers found the egg, and something damp. I pulled out a small scrap of yellow plastic rope and a feather which must have been recently floating—a few tiny pelagic barnacles clung to it. The parent must have had an urge, as hatching approached, to bring something, anything, from the sea. As I placed them back in the nest I heard voices. Sitting up, I looked around the deserted slopes. There they were again, words torn and fragmented by wind. Perhaps yachters or fishermen had arrived. The sound seemed to be coming from just over the rise. I got up and walked carefully between the burrows.

There was no one to be seen. Wind, stiff with the ammonia smell of guano, gusted up rock face. The cormorants flew off. Disappointed as I was, I laughed at myself for having been fooled by them again. I sat down to wait for their return.

There were less than a hundred pairs of pelagic cormorants nesting on the cliffs of Triangle Island. In June, after placing ragged little piles of eelgrass and seaweed nests on their narrow perches, three to five pale blue eggs appeared. The pair shared incubation. When one returned to the nest from the sea it flew towards the cliff, opening its wings up and back, and stretching out its webbed feet. It landed precariously on the ledge, fighting for balance before rubbing bills, entwining necks, and conversing with its mate.

On the water, cormorants are so silent I never imagined they could make such curious sounds. In their colonies they sound like trumpets and kazoos, fighting cats, and dogs defending a stick. Their strangled voices rise and fall as if they were struggling to speak, as if they had lost their tongues.

The Tlingit believed it was the trickster, Raven, who robbed Cormorant of his tongue. When Raven bragged of his prowess as a fisherman, the people asked for proof, pointing to rich halibut grounds nearby. Raven set off for them with Cormorant, commanding him to fill the boat with fish. Worried that Cormorant would tell the villagers about his laziness, Raven asked him, "What is that on your tongue?" When the puzzled Cormorant showed him his tongue, Raven quickly pulled it out. Cormorant, his ability to speak lost forever, could only listen while Raven regaled the villagers with tales of his own strength and skill.

Raven couldn't have picked a better fisherman to do his work for him. Cormorants are superb divers. Their large thigh muscles power feet that propel them more than forty yards deep. Their outer feathers, more "wettable" than those of many birds, compress to make them less buoyant. When they surface they must spread their wings to dry. Below me, three birds perched on a log, wings open—a floating line of black crosses.

I scanned the cliffs. Here the tide went up and down rather than in and out. This was land remote as air—reached only on the wing.

Around the corner from this face was a far noisier colony. The din of it rose like city traffic from the canyons between skyscrapers, a cacophony day and night. I walked toward it and lay on my stomach, leaning over the lip of the cliffs, holding tightly onto tufts of grass with both fists and digging my toes into the earth. Below me over 3,000 birds, jammed shoulder to shoulder, gabbled with their neighbours. Every toehold was occupied by sleek birds with white breasts and black backs—a massive, vertical cocktail party. On the water, more birds clustered in tight rafts.

They were common murres, among the biggest of the Alcidae or auk family, which includes the puffins. In May they began arriving by the thousands, vying for a few square inches of space on the wall. If we looked carefully we could find a few of the very similar thick-billed murres. Teetering on their tiny ledges, the male murres threw their heads back, pointing their long slender bills at the sky. Courting pairs preened and bowed to each other ceaselessly.

They had begun to lay in the last week—on each ledge was a beautiful turquoise egg with dark spots and squiggles. I recognized the egg I had seen on the window ledge the day I arrived on the island. The slight difference in colour and the distinctive pattern of marks on each egg help the parents recognize their own among thousands. The pear-shaped egg fits snugly under the brood patch, as the parent incubates, balancing it with its feet. If the egg is knocked, it tends to rock in a circle rather than away (and off the cliff), as a rounder egg would. For extra strength, the shell thickens at the end and where it contacts rock. Eventually it becomes covered with sticky guano. Within the porous egg, the chick grows, and memorizes the calls of its parents. Adults learn to recognize their own chicks, but new chicks respond to their parents' voices as soon as they hatch.

Before it can fly, a murre chick will begin to pace the edge of its ledge, squeaking and peering down at the sea, where adults answer with low growls. Less than half-grown it will be safer on

the last ISLAND

Common Murre on its single egg

the water than the cliff face where predators are constantly on the prowl. After dusk one evening, it takes a leap of faith, jumps into space, spreads its tiny wings and falls hundreds of feet to the water. If it hits rock, it simply bounces off, like a feather powderpuff. Two or three adults swim over protectively. If a predator swoops, they dive, the chick immediately mimicking them. Escorted by its male parent, which will teach it to hunt, it paddles out to sea.

As I watched the murres jostling on their ledges, it was possible to think of Triangle Island as a highrise where birds divide nesting habitat among themselves, from penthouse to basement suites. Among the six species of alcids, common murres lay claim to cliffs; tufted puffins, burrows on high, steep, open slopes. Rhinoceros auklets nest in burrows on lower, gentler slopes; Cassin's auklets in burrows on virtually all accessible parts of the island, including dense thickets; pigeon guillemots lay their eggs in deep cracks between rocks and boulders at the water's edge.

Over the summer Anne and I had seen a few horned puffins.

We had been watching them closely, to see if they had nests deep in the cracks halfway up the cliffs on Puffin Rock, where they usually landed. They had a small "horn" above the eye and slightly different beak coloration than the Atlantic puffin. Otherwise the species looked so similar they might have trouble telling each other apart. They would most likely not have to—auks move between the oceans only rarely.

The birds, which so adeptly divided up the windy cliffs and slopes below me, were an example of "adaptive radiation," a group of closely related species evolved from a common ancestor. And like Darwin's finches, each had a beak to go with its particular lifestyle.

When Anne and I captured Cassin's auklets in mist nets on our nocturnal forays we had seen their broad fleshy tongues, for capturing plankton, and the throat pouches in which they carried them back to their chicks.

We often watched the common murres, the most penguin-like of the alcids, diving deep for small fish in the waters close to their cliffs. Compared to puffins their bills are narrow and elegant. Their slender tongues are encased in a tough, horny shield to hold slippery fish against the ridges of their palates.

Like Cassin's auklets, puffins can feed on plankton, but during the breeding season, like murres, they hunt for small fish. Not surprisingly, their beaks are intermediate in design. The extravagant size and colour is mainly cosmetic. Inside, the beak is neither narrow nor wide. The tongue is hard only on its tip and not on the upper surface. When a fish is caught it is moved back and held against the palate—armed with backwards pointing spines or denticles—by the strong fleshy tongue. This is what allows them to carry so many fish at once. One Atlantic puffin was recorded to have 62 small fish in one load! However, they were very small—the total weight was less than a fifth of an ounce. If the fishing is good, a puffin will bring fewer, more nutritious, heavier fish; for instance, five or six in a load of almost an ounce, three or four times a day.

Above me the puffins winged quietly in from the sea. Nearby, murres dropped noisily from the cliff face. Far below I could see pigeon guillemots gathered in their customary conventions, calling wheezily amongst themselves on boulders at the water's edge.

Together, the species of birds in the alcid family have an appeal best understood by the passionate collector—ingenious elaboration on a single design.

July 20

Anne and I could only guess what kind of fish the puffins were bringing from the sea. As we took turns observing the returning birds, we recorded their disappearance into the burrows with their deliveries. We knew from other studies, which used infrared cameras, that when an adult enters the burrow chamber it utters a soft, clicking call. The hungry chick, which has been plaintively crying, emerges from the dark recesses. It pecks at and takes a few fish dangling from the bill of the parent, who then drops the lot on the earth.

Hoping that each chick was getting enough to grow on, we kept an eye out for gull pirates. The gulls had their own hungry chicks to feed. They were two weeks old—like spotted balls of dryer lint on long black legs. They waited inside the magic radius of their grass nests, having learned that if they wandered into their neighbour's territory a strange adult gull would strike at them angrily. When their own parent arrived the chicks pecked madly at the red spot on the end of its beak. As if a "vomit button" had been pushed, the parent regurgitated food.

One morning as I was absorbed with recording deliveries during the rush hour just after sunrise, a gull scream on the far edge of the colony surprised me. I leaned out of the blind to see what the commotion was. An adult gull swooped down just as a puffin landed. As the puffin desperately scrambled over the slope, the gull grabbed its tail in its beak and yanked hard. The startled puffin flapped its wings and ducked into its burrow, dropping its fish. The gull quickly relinquished the tail, snatched up the fish, and flew off. Though both Anne and I saw some attempts, most gulls didn't pursue the puffins with much conviction.

Anne needed to know what types of fish the adults were bringing from the sea. Though we tried a few times to check a burrow as soon as the adult left, we could never get to the fish before the young had gobbled them up.

Anne spent hours trying to devise some way of keeping the

Part One

Glaucous-winged gull chick just hatched. We could hear peeping in the next egg

chick from eating the fish before we got there. We thought of hoods, but were worried that it would distress the adult if the chick's head was covered. She tried making something that would simply keep the chick from opening its beak.

One afternoon as I came in from my shift in the blind, she held up a tangle of string and electrician's tape.

"I think this might work," she said.

"What is it?" I asked, baffled.

"It's a tiny muzzle." She showed me how it could be fitted over the chick's beak, stretched over the back of the head and tightened with the string.

Early the next morning we climbed the trail to Puffin Rock together. We gently pulled a chick from one of our burrows. It struggled, pushing at us with the little claws of its webbed feet, flapping its stubby, unfeathered wings, and snapping ineffectually as we fit the contraption over its beak, which had not yet shed the pale knob of egg tooth.

We crawled to the blind and sat quietly, waiting for its next food delivery. The adult stayed longer than usual in the nest. When it emerged and flew off to sea we returned to the burrow. We could hear the chick peeping. Anne pulled it out and untied the muzzle. I felt around in the dark, until my hand found a little pile of cold, slippery fish.

Anne gave a little cry of delight, "Voila!"

I looked at the seafood in my hand. I had no idea what they were: three slender, silver fish, dusted with earth, and about as long as my palm.

"These are probably sandlance," Anne said, picking them up and running her finger over the gleaming scales. Her nails were broken like mine, with permanent crescents of dirt under them. She pulled a grimy cotton bag and some scales out of her pack and dropped the fish in the bag. As she jotted down their description and weight, I placed them back in the burrow.

This meal had probably been caught in coastal waters. Tufted puffins do not fly far out to sea to forage for their young. They can fly fast—Atlantic puffins have been clocked at 51 miles per hour—but their bodies are heavy compared to their wings. Because they must beat them over 300 times per minute, flying takes a lot of energy.

The fish that the puffins bring home were the ones they could snatch from the upper waters. Each day there is not only an ebb and flood of the tide on the shore, but living tides below the surface. Fish and plankton move in vertical columns, up to the surface, and back down into deeper layers. Moving towards or away from the light, some rise during the day, some at night, like passengers in glass elevators. Any fish that descend during the day will not be available to puffins, who always fish the day shift. They will, however, be targets for nocturnal birds like rhinoceros auklets.

Puffins deliver many different things to their young: squid, young rockfish, and Pacific sauries. One summer the bluethroat Argentine, a fish usually found in deep, cold offshore waters, suddenly turned up in puffin meals. On islands closer to shore puffins often fish for herring. In Alaska, capelin is a large part of their summer menu. But nothing is more important to them up and down the coast than Pacific sandlance.

Each day these fish wriggle out of sand, where they have buried themselves for the night, and join thousands of their kind, rising to feed on plankton. Puffins dive after them. Underwater, the logic of the puffins' awkward physique is revealed: the sleek body is driven by paddle-like wings, slightly bent at the "wrist"; the feet act as rudders, and the birds appear to "fly" underwater. The sandlance flash like quicksilver in the morning light, the smaller fish on the edge of the school veering frantically away from the nimble puffins; in the center swim the larger fish, protected by the swarming confusion around them.

But puffins are not the sandlance's only worry. Sandlance are one of the staples of the north Pacific banquet, relished by pelagic cormorants, sooty shearwaters, cod, halibut, sole, salmon, seals, sea lions, minke, sei, and humpback whales. All summer, if they manage to survive their many predators, the sandlance fatten on plankton. Fish of the continental shelf, Pacific sandlance are rarely found in water over 300 feet deep. As the summer light wanes, they drop to the bottom, and bury themselves in sand until the next spring.

July 25

Anne was more and more focussed on her research. Chick feeding and growth rates were the summer's most important data. They had to be collected carefully and consistently. Each evening after we cleared away dinner, she carefully copied out our field notes. I tried to read scientific papers but it became harder and harder for me to concentrate on data. I ended up staring out the window at the waves.

Alone on the colony I sat in the blind, forcing myself to watch each burrow diligently for puffins arriving with food, and make pencil entries in my notebook: 6:57 a.m., burrow SS 13, 7:05, burrow SS 08. But my mind wandered. It was as if the sheer space around me spun my thoughts outwards. Each day I spent more and more time thinking about less and less.

After three hours of observation I visited each burrow. If a parent had dropped off fish that morning I pulled them out,

fishing in the rain...

Part One

Anne with a two week old puffin chick

described and weighed them. I found the chick and removed the muzzle I had tied on it before sunrise. Its beak free, it greeted me with fierce peeps and pecks, quieting only when I tucked it inside the comforting darkness of the weighing bag. It struggled again as I took it out. I opened its wing like a fan to measure with calipers the length of the primary feathers that pushed through short, stiff sheaths bristling along the edge of its wings. Its body was covered with sooty down. Its eyes, beak and legs were black. Its feet were large. I stretched the thin, strong, webbed foot open, looking for ticks, hanging like ripe fruit, darkly engorged with blood. I picked them off and crushed them with my calipers.

   I knew by heart each of our 78 burrows on four plots: which parents had mysteriously lost eggs early in the season and re-laid, which nests had been abandoned, which chicks were strong and healthy, which were runts.

   I yawned, tired from my early morning work, and crawled from one burrow to another until all twenty burrows on the observation plot had been visited. Then I gathered up notebook, backpack and my scattered thoughts and went home for breakfast and a nap.

July 26

"Hello," I said, cheerily, as Anne came in from her morning shift. It was a warm sunny day, and I was stretched out, writing in my journal after a morning of preserving and labelling fish samples.

Anne didn't look at me, or smile.

"The fish samples are all done," I said, wondering if she thought I should have been busy, rather than lying on my bunk. I got up and pointed to the plastic vials lined up along the table.

She glanced at them dismissively, silently unpacking her gear. Something was wrong.

"What is it?" I sat up and closed my journal.

"A chick was dead this morning," she said flatly. "When I went to burrow 16 this morning, the chick still had its muzzle on." She finally looked at me. "You forgot to take it off."

I searched my mind, grabbed my notebook and flipped it to yesterday's page. Burrow 15 was the last entry on the previous page. I had skipped straight to 17—burrow 16's data was missing. I slumped down on my bunk.

I thought of the parents faithfully dropping fish at the feet of the chick, starving, unable to eat. The painful death I had inflicted on the innocent bird sickened me. I imagined the parents returning to the empty nest for the next few days, before finally abandoning it and returning to the sea. It was too late in the season for them to lay another egg.

Anne turned away, set her notebook on the table and began hanging up scales and calipers. All the information we had collected on that nest—position and length, date of laying, weekly weights of egg, date of hatching, weights and wing lengths of the chick—was wasted. We had had to discard our work before— several burrows had lost eggs and chicks just around the time of hatching. Though we didn't understand them, they were natural losses. This loss would never have occurred if I weren't here.

"Look, Anne, I really am sorry." As I spoke to her back, her shoulders stiffened.

She turned, reproachfully. "Sometimes I think the research isn't important to you. You don't try to be careful."

She was right; I was always daydreaming, and in a hurry to finish my work.

Resentfulness rose above self-reproach. "I *do* care about the birds. But I'm not like you."

"You still have to try to do a good job."

Self-pity overwhelmed me and tears rolled down my cheeks. I wanted someone to put an arm around my shoulder, tell me that it was okay, that everyone makes mistakes. Anne turned away, sat down at the counter and began to copy out the morning's data.

July 30

The next morning, the events of the day before settled heavily on me as soon as I opened my eyes. I was empty. How would I survive another month?

Anne was up. I dressed lethargically, glancing out the window at rain. I pulled on damp socks and shuffled into the kitchen. Anne was pouring coffee. She turned and offered me the cup she had just filled.

"I had strange dreams last night," she said. "I had to go back to Vancouver to get a radio but I couldn't get to the helicopter, which landed in my back yard. I got caught in a parade. I was worried that you were here alone, and that I couldn't return to finish my work." She rolled her eyes and laughed.

"Anne," I said. "I feel bad about the chick…"

She stirred her coffee. "It's okay. We still have lots of chicks to study."

"Thanks," I said, putting my hand on her arm briefly. She looked up, smiling slightly, and shrugged.

The chicks grew quickly. So far this summer the birds were finding the fish. For puffins, every summer is a gamble in which they must hit the jackpot for a few short weeks or lose their chicks. Safe from most predators on their remote colonies, their challenge is to find the food moving in the vast, three-dimensional world of water stretching out around them. Unlike the albatross patrolling the far corners of the ocean to feed its chick, puffins are pinned by their small wings to the waters within several miles of the island. If the fishing is good, a chick doubles its weight a week after hatching. By two weeks old it is five times heavier. By the time it fledges it is almost as big as its parent, weighing almost a pound.

common murre colony -
gulls patrolling edges,
waiting for a chance to
scavenge

Some summers the fish are just not there. Sometimes the prey is too big for the chick to get down. Sometimes it is a jellyfish, which has little nutritional value. In those years the chicks grow slowly. Many do not fledge. Occasionally a deep knowledge sweeps the colony and every bird abandons the nesting colony before the eggs even hatch. In 1976, during a summer of stormy weather, puffins deserted all over the island. Something had cued the birds, some signal so profound that they chose to conserve their energy and give up the entire season. The next year was also a difficult summer. Though the birds did not abandon, few chicks fledged.

Almost all seabirds face the problems of surviving in a capricious ocean. In some nesting seasons temperatures rise or fall, currents shift, unusual storms interfere with feeding, plankton and fish don't turn up where they are expected. Almost all seabirds have evolved a strategy to deal with the unpredictable nature of their home. Drawing their breeding chances out over many years, they live a long time and have only one chick per summer. Puffins, which can live twenty-five years, count on their long breeding lives to leave a few healthy offspring.

August 1

It was so hot when I came down from my shift in the blind at midday that even the frigid sea looked inviting. I stripped and jumped quickly into one of the deep pools in the reef below Puffin Rock.

Drying myself with my T-shirt, I noticed a seal frantically haul itself up onto a rock not far from me, its eyes wide and terrified. I scanned the quiet beach and empty sky. The bay was serene. The seal looked anxiously from me to the sea. Suddenly, a swimming pool's length away, the tip of a black fin broke the surface. It sliced through the water, slowly rising to its full height of about six feet. The whale took a single breath, water pouring off its dark back, and submerged, the fin sinking again. I stood with cold water dripping from my hair onto my bare shoulders, watching the spot where the animal had disappeared. A few seconds later it re-emerged with a quiet exhalation farther down the beach.

Part One

The seal looked nervously to the water, clearly weighing its options. It decided I was less frightening than the killer whale and stayed put.

I had seen orcas before. It was not uncommon to spot them in the summer from the ferries that cross between Vancouver Island and the mainland. Gathering in the narrow straits, which funnel fish around Vancouver Island to spawning grounds on great rivers like the Fraser, the killer whales travel in groups ranging from a few animals to fifty.

This whale was alone. I watched it slip around the far point of the island. As the seal's face told me, it was not hunting salmon. The dark knife of fin, its stealthy sweep of the shore, made me shiver.

When I was a child, the details of the killer whale's life were obscure. It was known that these toothed whales, actually the largest members of the dolphin family, were widely distributed in the world's oceans and had different dining habits depending on local food. The name "killer" came from observations, mostly by whalers, of groups attacking and eating other whales. "Indeed they may be regarded as marine beasts, that roam over every ocean; entering bays and lagoons, where they spread terror and death among the mammoth balaenas and the smaller species of dolphin," whaling captain Charles Scammon wrote in 1874.

The fear that our waters were teeming with killers relentlessly gorging on salmon led the Department of Fisheries and Oceans, in 1960, to install a machine-gun mount in Seymour Narrows, halfway down Vancouver Island's inner passage. Fisheries reports from the time suggest other "control" measures—depth charges, fragmentation bombs, dynamite and mortars. Though they were never used, nor the machine-gun ever fired, fishermen regularly shot at killer whales.

Not until the first killer whale was captured in the 1960s did aquaria discover they were docile and highly trainable animals. Overnight an industry grew on the BC and Washington coasts. Entrepreneurs set nets where whales were known to travel. The captured animals were transferred to holding pens, then sold to aquaria all over the world. Reclassified as a harvested animal, the killer whale became, for federal fisheries, an object of scientific research.

The first census, 15,000 questionnaires urging ferry operators and lightkeepers to record all killer whale sightings on one specific day in July, 1971, was surprising. The speed and range of their movements had created the false impression that there were thousands of whales. At best there were only about 350.

The researchers, led by a British Columbian scientist named Mike Biggs, set out to follow and photograph the groups at every opportunity. They soon discovered that, like people, each whale was different. They bore different markings, and their fins were unique in shape or characteristic nicks and scratches. After studying thousands of photos researchers were able to recognize each individual whale on the coast and learned that killer whales travelled in matriarchal family groups or pods. Calves, male or female, spent their whole lives with their mothers. What I had seen as a child were family picnics—serene matriarchs, exuberant juveniles, young females, brothers and uncles with muscular, towering dorsal fins—moving on predictable routes, sometimes coming together with other pods in their area. In the waters of Vancouver Island researchers recognized two communities. The northern group ranges from mid-Vancouver Island to the southeast tip of Alaska. The southern community plies the waters of southern Vancouver Island, reaching into Puget Sound and around the coast of Washington state to Grays Harbour. They do not swim into each others' waters. Though they disappear mysteriously in the winter, the researchers called them "resident" whales because of their summer habits.

It was soon discovered that these highly social whales used diverse and complex sounds, or echolocation, with each other, especially when hunting schools of salmon. Each pod and each community's voice was distinctive, its own dialect of squeaks, ticks, clicks and whines.

Research revealed the unexpected: there were other whales—animals that travelled farther, faster, and often alone or in very small groups. They did not eat salmon, and did not swim with, converse with, or mate with the salmon-eating whales. Almost silent, they were aquatic stalkers, hunters of marine mammals like seals and young sea lions. They became known as "transient" whales.

Myths and carvings of the Kwakiutl tell how intimately they

Part One

Bull kelp
Nereocystis luetkeana

observed these animals. They knew that killer whales travelled long distances, believing them to live at the outer side of the world, an ocean journey of four days.

The little seal jelly-rolled back down the beach and ducked back into the water. If the transient had surprised him he would not have lasted long. Salmon-eating resident whales are carnivores at a tea party, compared to transients. The killer whale's powerful jaws, lined with forty interlocking, curving teeth almost five inches long, can finish off a seal or sea lion pup in a few bites.

As I pulled on my damp T-shirt and gathered up my pack, a puffin flew overhead, pumping its little black wings earnestly, fish in its beak flashing like tinsel. I picked up my notebook and flipped quickly through the mud-streaked pages. It was almost full. There were columns of measures on burrows, degree of slope, soil depth and length. Then came egg lengths, widths and weights, followed by chick hatching weights, wing lengths and finally numbers, types, and weights of fish delivered. Since the muzzle incident and the death of the chick, I had forced myself to attend to my job carefully. Any bright notions I had once about the romance of being a field biologist had tarnished. But I understood how important the tedious work was. I thought about the thousands of photographs of killer whales, the hours and hours of underwater recordings that had to be collected before animals thought to be vicious, indiscriminate predators were understood to be highly evolved groups as tightly bound as a human family. Only chapter after plodding chapter of data had revealed the bigger story.

On the beach in front of our trailer, greasy smoke rose in a plume that was pulled offshore and frayed by the wind. Anne was standing beside a fire, burning garbage, tossing cardboard and paper onto the flame.

"Did you see the whale?" I called.

"What whale?" She scanned the bay, excited. We had been waiting since our sighting of fin whales to get another good look at whales. I described to her the transient's lone sweep of our shore, and the frightened seal, his beguiling face and round dark eyes. I was sympathetic to the seal, but secretly I wished the whale had been successful in his hunt, so that I could have witnessed the terrifying negotiations between life and death—the moment of predation.

August 5

Imperceptibly, the sun began to wind the light back in. Strange birds appeared. A Swainson's thrush skulked in a tangle of salmonberry. It was a bird I knew well; its slightly off-key, upward spiralling song evoked the deep coast forest of other summers. One afternoon, an exhausted-looking, violet-green swallow landed on the roof of the trailer. In the bay, a dozen harlequin ducks snorkelled along the surf line. They were joined, for a few days, by a small group of green-winged teal. One morning we woke to find a great blue heron on our beach, calmly preening his silk cravat of breast feathers. Every day, more shorebirds alighted: a whimbrel picked through seaweed with its long, curved bill, a dark knot of black turnstones landed on the point east of our beach, and wandering tattlers flew up and down the shore, their calls like electronic alarm clocks.

The short summer was over for birds of the far north. Millions of birds were already winging south. One day the sky conjured a flock of dainty birds, flashing white then disappearing as they turned in faultlessly synchronized flight. They circled and suddenly settled like scraps of paper in a windy street. I quickly lifted my binoculars to see a small contingent of western sandpipers. Most of the world's population of this species pours down the Pacific flyway each spring. They must have sighted the island from above and dropped in.

They dashed along, rifling through the tideline. But Triangle's rocky shores were slim pickings. Sandpipers prefer mud flats where they stir the sediments and pull up tiny crabs, worms and shrimps with their tweezer-like beaks. Chances are these birds were not yet expert at finding ideal pit stops—they were only about a month old. Shortly after they had hatched, in July, their mothers left the breeding grounds in western Alaska for the shores of Central and South America. A week later the males had followed, leaving the chicks to feed alone. Weighing no more than a mouse, the chicks had started their first flight south, unguided, carrying a mysterious internal map and a tiny reserve of tangerine-coloured fat in a cuplike depression between the wishbones. Winds had provided the rest of the fuel. The birds can climb as high as 20,000 feet, where the atmosphere thins and becomes turbulent. The next day, our visitors were gone, surfing the winds south.

As the summer ripened, birds grew plump as fruit and the sea began its harvest. Each night, while we slept, chicks tumbled from burrows, crawling and flapping down the island's slopes, and over the dark beach. Some never made it.

One morning Anne and I found a Cassin's auklet chick so weak that it couldn't stand. I picked it up. It did not have the energy for even a half-hearted peck. Its eyes were half-closed.

"What do you think?" I held it out and Anne took it from me, holding it close and checking it for injuries. One wing wouldn't

Lesser Yellowlegs
just passing through on the way from nesting areas in the far north to wintering grounds in South America

fan out properly. It had a raw red wound on the underside.

"This is probably a broken wing," she frowned and walked to the water's edge, her gumboots slapping against her strong calves. I looked down at my own legs, white between the gumboots and shorts, like Anne's. It had not been warm enough for us to wear shorts often, so despite four months outdoors we had "farmers' tans," browned only on our faces, necks, and hands.

When Anne set the auklet down, it floated without paddling or scrambling back to shore.

"He's done for, if he doesn't start to swim," I said, stepping to the water, bending down and tapping his tail feathers to set him off in the right direction. We stood back and watched him hopelessly.

"He's probably done for, anyway," Anne said.

We both knew he was dying.

"Do you think he's suffering?" I wondered aloud. "Maybe it would be merciful to end it." He was so small, surely we could kill him quickly. The waves washed him back onto the shore like flotsam. Anne picked him up and held him for a moment. She snapped the head back, trying to break the neck. The bird peeped weakly.

"Here, I'll try," I said. I willed myself to twist hard on the neck, as fine as a twig under my fingers. But it was surprisingly strong.

A wave of disgust swept over me. "Anne, let's just let it die on its own." I set the bird down as gently as I could. I couldn't kill it with my bare hands. Every summer thousands of birds do not make it back to the sea. Chicks starve. Birds are killed by disease or taken on the wing by peregrine or eagle. We couldn't begin to help the weak and dying in a colony of a million seabirds. But here, death's edges blurred—what wasn't hunted was scavenged, greedily brought back to life.

August 10

It took longer and longer each day to fill our water container. The spring that flowed from the base of the slope onto the beach shrank to a trickle. Finally, we had to set our container under it in the morning, propped in place with beach stones. Hours later, on our way back from the colonies, we picked it up.

After several days of this we were both stricken with fatigue and nausea and realized that our water, filtered through earth crammed with birds for months, was probably contaminated. We now boiled it, and used saltwater for almost everything except drinking. Bathing became an art, using less and less water, until we were down to a few cups a week. We set a tarp over the roof, but it didn't rain. I longed for the endless deluges of May.

I balanced on the rock, watching water rise around it, waiting for the perfect moment. If I timed it right I wouldn't have to wade in past my ankles for a quart of seawater. I quickly dipped the pot and jumped beyond the reach of tide, spilling a cup of cold water down my boot, soaking my wool sock. Quietly cursing, I limped up the beach, careful not to lose any of what remained in the pot. I was tired from a long day of work and didn't want to make the trek back to the shore. We would use this water to cook our noodles, wash our dishes, and brush our teeth.

I remembered the shock of my first mouth of seawater as a child, the bitterness I was not prepared for when I dove into what seemed like an endless lake. Only later I understood that the sea, seasoned with minerals eroded from rock by eons of rain and carried by rivers, is about 2.5 percent sodium chloride (good old table salt) and one percent other minerals. There is enough salt in it to cover all the continents in a layer five hundred feet thick. Until we became adept at purifying it, salt was precious. It was often traded ounce for ounce for gold.

Strangely, the people of the west coast of Vancouver Island did not relish salt. When the captain of the American ship *Boston* entertained Chief Maquinna and his retinue in Friendly Cove, in 1803, he found they could not endure the taste of it.

I thought of our trickle of freshwater growing thinner every day and was reminded how ill-adapted we were to this island. The plants were drying, clenching their fists of seeds, season's tickets to next summer. Land birds like thrushes and warblers were already leaving the island. The puffins were unperturbed. Somehow they survived on water three times saltier than their blood.

If Anne and I drank seawater we would produce a cup and a half of urine for every cup we swallowed. Seabirds survive without fresh water because of a pair of crescent-shaped glands nestled between their eyes, which absorb and pump salt away from the net of blood vessels surrounding them. A puffin can eliminate very salty water within twenty minutes, in droplets seven times as salty as tears.

A song sparrow fluttered up the beach in front of me, picking beach hoppers from piles of seaweed. Could I hold it in my hand if I salted its tail, as the old wives' tale promises? The sparrow flew off nervously. I turned and watched it land near the shore. Beyond the breaking surf the bay was innocent blue, the sky gazing fixedly at itself in its saltwater mirror.

August 20

I couldn't find the chick in burrow ER19 anywhere. I felt around the damp earth in all his usual haunts: the blind end left of the entrance, the little chamber beyond, and finally the very back of the passage, which I could only reach by lifting a plug of earth excavated early in the season. The burrow was empty. My heart sank. What could have happened to him? In the last week he had weighed in at a robust 13.26 ounces. Almost all his down was gone, except for a few wispy plumes around his neck. The rest of his dark plumage was sleek and his wing feathers were full grown and ready for flight. Suddenly I realized that he had probably fledged. We had lost this bird to the sea. I sat for a moment absorbing this. I had known this chick intimately, had noted when his parents laid their egg forty-five days ago and had cradled it in my palm, carefully weighing and measuring it. I had held him hours after hatching and recorded his favourite foods. Each day I drew him from his nest relieved to find him alive and healthy. But I had not seen him leave. I looked at my watch—10:17 a.m. By now he was probably miles away.

Like most seabirds, puffins make their first journey to the sea in the dark. They pace restlessly near the entrance of their burrow for several nights before they leave. Parents may stop feeding or even desert their chicks to push them out of the nest. At the very least the birds lose their enthusiasm for parenting in the last days before fledging, visiting the burrow less frequently, becoming less demonstrative and indulging in more social visits with other adults. Feeding may fall off so that the young do not weigh

almost ready to fledge...

too much when they fledge. They need to have enough reserves to carry them over their first clumsy days as hunters, but not so much fat that it is difficult to dive.

Once a chick leaves its burrow, it never returns. Soon after nightfall, it steps out for the first and last time, waddling over the hummocky ground, following the downward slope to the cliff edge. Without pausing it falls into space, with only fluttering wings and soft breast feathers to cushion its landing. Once it is swimming it may sip water and wash itself vigorously at the surface, but almost immediately it sets off to the open sea, diving and paddling. Unlike the half-grown murre chicks, it is not accompanied by a parent; young puffins encounter the sea alone.

Puffins disperse as if they had been shaken out of the sky, across the north Pacific. Possibly, young birds wander farthest—birds from Europe and Iceland, found off the Newfoundland coast, are usually first-year birds.

I thought about my chick paddling tirelessly since long before dawn—the unwavering determination of birds can seem like a kind of faith. I searched the empty horizon through my binoculars, silently wishing him well. If he survived the trials of his journey to sea and the dangers that awaited—storms, unpredictable food, predators, fishing nets and pollution—he could be back on Triangle Island in four or five years to nest on the slopes where he was born.

August 22

"Okay then, see you next week. I love you more than ten sockeye salmon."

Anne and I rolled our eyes, wondering what the reply was on the other end of the radio. The fisherman had requested "privacy" from the operator—only his wife could hear him. All that eavesdroppers could hear was a monotonous beeping.

This new radio had arrived by yet another helicopter a few days before. Someone had finally realized that our previous radio had the wrong crystals for transmitting and receiving so far offshore. The answer was a marine radio, issued to boats. Now we were the good ship *Puffin*. Listening to fishermen on the radiophone had become our after-dinner entertainment.

With my thumb poised on the mike, I waited for the moment I could jump into the busy traffic to place my own call to Steven. Strangely, I wasn't anxious to get through. Accustomed to solitude, I no longer desperately missed him.

August 25

I stuck my head out the door. To our relief it had been raining for two days, filling our tarp and feeding the spring down the beach. But today we were hoping for good weather. With fewer and fewer chicks to monitor, Anne decided we could take a final day off. Slender white clouds scored the clear sky.

From behind the trailer, we started the long scramble to the saddle of the island. I remembered the first time we had made this climb. That day in early May seemed a lifetime ago. The storms of spring were long past. Summer had come and was almost gone. The puffins had courted, nested, incubated eggs and raised chicks. Anne and I had spent almost four months working and living with only each other.

We crested the island's flank and began pushing our way through dense, wind-pruned salmonberry and crabapple. Above us the lighthouse stared with its blind eye. It was not our destination today. We wanted to get to the beach on the north shore—the beach by which the lighthouse people arrived and left, long ago.

We slid down the steep drop, clutching at grass. Stone headlands rose on either end of the bay. Seals lounged on reefs like burly mermaids. Cobblestones clattered in the surf. Resting on the beach, we passed the water bottle back and forth, talking of the future. In a week I would be leaving for school. Anne would stay on with another research assistant for a couple more weeks, to see the puffins off. More and more burrows were empty in the mornings when we climbed to the colonies. By mid-September almost all of the chicks would be gone.

"When I get back, come to my house for dinner. I'll cook something fresh," Anne laughed. She had turned out to be a more inspired cook than I.

After all the meals we had shared, it would be strange to sit down across the table from someone else. I stared at the beach, trying to remember what life was like beyond this island.

Part One

Something in the beach sand caught my eye—the gleam of mother of pearl. We stretched out on our stomachs, and began to pick shells like flowers. Some were as big as soup bowls, shallow and glazed with iridescence. Along one edge was a neat line of five holes, where water would flow out of the animal after it had passed over its gills.

"I've never seen such big abalone shells." I said, setting them in a pile beside me. "I'll take these home as souvenirs, since I never found a glass ball."

I had given up hope of finding one, after looking diligently all summer. Today I would not be any luckier—anything fragile would have been dashed on these rocks.

Anne dug Ricketts out of her pack to look up a small snail with fluted whorls. But she didn't tuck any shells away for herself—she would be back next year, and probably the year after that. It would take more than one summer for her to complete her work. Studying birds requires the patience of a farmer. The work cannot unfold faster than the seasons.

I realized how little time I had left here. A bittersweet feeling, like nostalgia for the present, swept over me. The hard stone that I had carried for months—my resistance to the island's isolation and uncompromising wildness—dissolved.

A raven flew over, folding in his wings and flipping, so that for an instant he was flying upside down, belly to the sky. Then, so swiftly that I couldn't see if he did a full barrel roll or a half turn, he flipped right side up again, as if he was performing for us. I understood why, for so many of the coastal people, Raven was a clever trickster. He was also a powerful being: emerging from antediluvian darkness, he stole the sun from the woman who kept it locked in a box, and released the daylight. Before long he had secured the tides, obtained fire, created salmon, liberated herring and painted the birds.

The raven repeated his acrobatics, pumped his wings and flew on with a throaty *quork, quork*, a call I had never heard. Raven voices are boxes with rusty hinges, full of knocks, croaks and rattling pebbles. Boas describes how the Kwakiutl believed that if a child's afterbirth were left on the beach for the ravens to peck at, the grown child would be able to understand the birds' language and pass on to his tribe valuable advice about hunting prospects or the arrival of warring parties. The Kwakiutl all recognized some raven sounds. I wondered whether what I heard as *quork quork* would be *Sox sox sox* to their ears. This meant the weather would be calm and sunny, as it was today; *wax wax wax* told that a stranger would soon arrive. When a raven cried *xagaq xagaq*, a woman would soon die.

The raven called one last time and disappeared around the next point, where an answering call echoed off Triangle's cliffs.

August 28

After dinner we took our tea, our last bottle of rum, and a pan of bannock batter down to the beach. We crouched over our fire pit, feeding a tiny teepee of twigs and paper carefully until the fire burned bright. I rocked back and forth, making a cradle for my body in the cool stones, and reclined against a beach log, enjoying the familiar sharp smell of salt-soaked wood smoke. I poured a shot of our rum (which had been replenished by the last chopper trip) into a cup of tea and handed it to Anne. She set the bannock near the fire, waiting for hot coals, and stretched out opposite me. As the sky darkened, we fell into comfortable silence, watching the smoke rise through the steam from our tea. The white line of surf zipped and unzipped the shore. Over our heads, the first rhinoceros auklets began their nightly circling.

The days, which had seemed so long when I first arrived on the island, were passing more and more quickly. They had worn Triangle's sharp edges into something like home. I looked across at Anne who was staring at the fire, lost in thought. The months had made her face familiar in its smallest detail: pale freckles, narrow, straight nose, full lips, blond cap of curls. Though I hadn't noticed it happening, we had come to know each other well. The summer had worn away the edges of our differences into friendship. She glanced up and smiled.

"This must be hot enough by now," she said, leaning forward and balancing the frying pan on two logs.

We talked idly about camping as children. *"Fire's burning, fire's burning, draw nearer, draw nearer, in the glowing, in the glowing, come sing and be merry,"* I sang, remembering the corny old campfire song from summer camp. Anne tried to teach me her version: "*Feu, feu, joli feu, ta chaleur nous éblouit, feu, feu, joli feu, danse dans la nuit.*" After stumbling through it a few times, laughing, we fell silent again, watching the fire and dodging smoke as the wind shifted restlessly.

I leaned my head back and looked at the glittering stars above me. In Kwakiutl myth the sky was a country in the house of the sun, which could be reached only through a small hole in the western horizon, or by flying across or diving under a high mountain. It was the home of many ancestors who lived as birds.

I untangled the dazzling array, following the line of the Big Dipper to thread the pole star's white needle. Wheeling around it was Draco, its sinuous body winding through the crowded sky like a dragon dancer, and the Pleiades' small, bright cluster, a diamond brooch, pinned low in the north. I remembered that these familiar stars were ghost images, their light lapping this shore like a swell that has taken millions of years to cross a vast sea.

I searched for one of my favourite constellations, a tiny arc of stars frozen in a dolphin's leap. Delphinus swam just outside the luminous wake of the Milky Way, on the northern edge of the part of the sky known as the Heavenly Waters. Spilling into the southern hemisphere were constellations I had never seen, named by Europeans when they first sailed into the southern oceans: whales, sea monsters, and fish gleamed in that sky like bioluminescent creatures of the abyss.

I pushed at the coals with a piece of driftwood and orange sparks spiralled up in the smoke. Fire is constant. I had circled the sun twenty-three times, living on its charity, my own metabolism nothing but cellular fire—oxygen consuming the stuff of stars. Beyond our amber circle of light, life was ignited as if by some great act of arson: the sea burned with plankton and whales, the island smouldered with fireweed and salmonberries. In the darkness above me, the air was flaming with wings.

September 1

I woke in the middle of the night from a restless sleep, with moonlight pouring through my little window. If the clear sky held, the pilot would have no problem making it to Triangle in the morning. I lay listening to the surf, the heartbeat of the island. I wondered if I would wake in my home in the city, feeling something was wrong; something was missing.

I was up first for a change, and making coffee. After breakfast I packed my things as Anne prepared a few boxes of books, nets, and tools to send out early. We worked efficiently, having learned over the months how to move around each other in the tiny space. By 10:30 I was ready. The helicopter wasn't due until noon, so I decided to stroll to the base of Puffin Rock one last time.

As I began walking, I imagined the journey ahead of me today, reeling me in, across sea and sky, along highway. I stood looking up at the trail I had first climbed with such trepidation. It was well worn now by hundreds of trips up and down it. High above me puffins were coming and going, absorbed, as always, with living.

When I returned we carried gear to the little landing pad, overgrown with nettles. A faint thrum broke into a deafening pounding, which echoed off the parabola of land, as the helicopter appeared over the ridge and dropped toward us. In the back window I could see the face of Jane, the woman who would help Anne for the next two weeks. She looked astonished. I remembered the first time I had seen Triangle's barren cliffs rising out of the sea.

The machine landed and the pilot leaped out with the blades still turning. This would be a short stop. He and Jane handed Anne and me a few boxes of supplies before we quickly started to load our own baggage.

"Oh, wait." Anne looked as if she had forgotten something and ran back to the trailer. She returned as I passed the pilot the last box.

I ducked under the blades and ran back to where she and Jane were standing at the edge of the clearing.

"Here."

She handed me her glass ball.

Part One

"Anne," I said, shaking my head. "You'll never find another one."

She shrugged and smiled.

"Thank you." I stepped towards her and for a moment we hugged each other hard. I climbed into the helicopter, fastened my seatbelt and put on my headphones. Suddenly the ground fell away, as if the island was leaving me behind, with only a bird's-eye view. As we turned I looked back. Anne stood shielding her eyes against the sun with one hand, and waving with the other, her figure getting smaller and smaller, until we passed over the island and she disappeared.

PART TWO

"He prayeth well, who loveth well
Both man and bird and beast"

Samuel Taylor Coleridge, *The Rhyme of the Ancient Mariner*

August 18, 1996

I had forgotten that the light here is unlike anywhere else, the way it pours from a wide open sky. In the dusk, the land and sea fade to the colours of a hand-tinted photograph. Looking through this window I am vividly aware of the years that have passed, each a road with fewer and fewer branches, where some things are kept and others fall away.

Hannah pulls me from my reverie. "When did you work here?" She slips off the edge of the bench we share and grabs the matches from beside the stove.

"Nineteen-eighty." I imagine how that must sound to her—it was only a few years after she was born. The past compresses—it doesn't seem very long ago that I was sitting here with Anne.

"Was it just you and Anne?" she asks as she lights a stub of candle stuck in an old soy sauce bottle. Yellow light flickers up and catches the faces around the table.

I nod, wondering if they know that Parks will no longer permit just two people to work here.

"You must have had so much room!" she laughs as she tries to wedge her legs under the table, among the tangle of limbs.

"I never thought of it that way. I was often lonely."

"What was she like?" Hannah leans forward, and pulls her hair off her forehead with one hand. I notice the familiar cracked, dirty fingernails.

How to describe someone in a few sentences? I see Anne mugging at our swimming hole, wrapped in yards of feather boa seaweed; I hear her singing along to our worn-out tapes, tripping over the lyrics. But mostly I remember a serious, dedicated woman. I cannot recall her mentioning that she ever wanted to be anything but a biologist. For her, that summer was an important beginning.

"She was small and strong and energetic. She was passionate about her work, never happier than when she was working in a puffin colony. She was…"

How to describe the odd intimacy the summer forged between us—as if we had shared a lifeboat.

"She was a good friend."

"Were you on the island when she died?" Laura pushes her

plate to the side, props her elbows on the table and rests her chin in her hands.

Everyone who comes to work on Triangle Island knows that Anne died here. It has become part of Triangle's dark lore.

"No, that was two years later."

I remembered the day I heard. That summer I was working for British Columbia Parks, on another island. It was not remote, so I could come out for time off. Before heading home for a few days I wandered into the office to pick up messages.

"Hey," one of the wardens called, just as I was going out the door. "Didn't you work on that Triangle Island place?"

"Yes." I stopped and looked back over my shoulder questioningly.

"Said on the news the other day that some woman was killed there. Fell off a cliff."

I remember hearing a Swainson's thrush in the nearby forest. Before it unravelled its thread of song, before I asked if he caught her name, I knew it was Anne.

August 19

First thing in the morning we set out, heading for this year's study sites on Puffin Rock. Laura strides on ahead. I walk less quickly, wanting to remember everything.

Puffin Rock basks in the morning sun, a magnificent sight and one that seems unreal at first, its monumental form materializing from the landscape of memory. Beyond it the sea is stiff with white caps. Oystercatchers fly up as we pass, whistling *kwee kwee kweeeee*. Just as I remembered them, a dozen seals watch our progress. Their faces have that curious, human expression that inspired the northern peoples to see seals as "selkies," gentle spirits longing for the world of men, able to shed their fur skins but always destined to return to their kin.

At the base of Puffin Rock I take a deep breath, snap on my hardhat and start to climb, holding on to a fixed rope in the sections that seem to cut straight up. By the time I get to the top, a half-hour later, I am panting and sweating. I can't believe that sixteen years ago Anne and I had bounded up it like goats, often twice a day.

We push our way through the salmonberry shrubs to the

grassy meadows of the puffin colonies. Anne's work suggested that, given a plentiful supply of fish, many things make for healthy chicks, including burrow site and parental experience. But like most biological research, her studies generated as many questions as they answered. Laura, Richard and Hanna are collecting data to find answers to some of those questions. Why do some eggs seem to disappear early in the season? What do the birds feed their young and how often? What are the chicks' growth rates?

Laura leads me to a slope where orange, purple and yellow surveying tape flutters from wooden stakes pushed into the soil at burrow entrances. We step carefully onto narrow terraces between the clumps of grass. I remember how easy it is to break through a roof, crushing the egg or bird below.

We stop at a burrow, marked 6A NE. Today we are going to weigh and measure the chick. I extend my arm into the entrance, confident that an adult, with its formidable bill, will not be waiting for me—by this time in the season the adults leave the chick to go fishing. I slip my hand into the dark damp burrow and close it over the small, feathered body of a puffin chick. As I gently pull it out and brush the soil from its breast, it looks up with fierce black, shiny eyes and tries to nip me with its tiny bill. It is sooty-coloured with a white chest. Pale grey down covers it like a shawl, forms a ruff around the neck, and a tuft on the rump.

Laura hands me the calipers and I measure the length of the outermost wing feather without thinking. We gently place the chick in a cotton bag and quickly weigh it with a small hanging scale. Chick 6A NE weighs 250 grams, just over half a pound. Laura sighs and pushes a stray strand of windblown hair out of her eyes.

"This is half what it should weigh at 45 days old. It's nearly time to fledge but the young that have made it this far are too small, have too much down and undeveloped flight feathers." A cloud passes over her sunny face. "Every day we watch chicks we have been weighing since they hatched grow weaker. Most days there is at least one burrow in the study plots where the chick has disappeared. Sometimes we find the body nearby. Last week we performed an autopsy on one chick. Its stomach was black."

"Why? " I ask.

"It was so hungry it ate earth."

She hands the bird to me and fishes a small metal band from her pocket.

"Pull the right foot down for me," she says. While the bird squirms, she slips the yellow band around the bird's spindly ankle then tightens it with a plier-like tool, checking to make sure it isn't too tight before she scribbles its number in her book. This is the identification bracelet that will reveal place and date of birth if this bird is found in future.

I move to return the chick to its burrow.

"Wait—one more thing." Laura pulls a small package from her pack and opens the plastic wrapping.

"Just hold the right wing open for me," she says, as she removes a tiny syringe and needle.

With a faint queasiness I realize she is going to take a blood sample. She grimaces as she quickly pierces the vein where it runs near the surface, on the underside of the wing bend. The chick squirms in my hand. The syringe fills quickly, Laura pulls out the needle and presses sterile gauze to the wing. When she removes it a moment later it is stained with a single red drop.

None of the researchers likes taking blood samples. It is hard to ignore the panic of the chick, especially if it takes more than one try to get the sample. I was thankful that I didn't have to do it during my summer here with Anne. But science has changed. Since I was a student, DNA analysis has become so fast and easy that studying almost every living thing includes probing the most intimate apparatus of its cells. This tiny vial of blood, taken back to the lab, holds volumes of information. A quick look at the bird's chromosomes can tell us what we could never know before, the sex of the chick. It can also identify fathers, mothers, sons and daughters. It can tell us about the evolutionary past and the movements of genes within and between populations today.

As we move through the colony I begin to notice dead chicks everywhere, lying at burrow entrances where they emerged out of desperation. They are desiccated by sun and wind. Crows and gulls wheel overhead. Quick to scavenge, they are already sated. This year the puffins are starving.

August 20

It begins as one of my recurring dreams. As always, I am in a small boat and it is sinking. This time it is a kayak that has sprung a leak. Slowly it fills with water, while I paddle as hard as I can until I come to a crowded dock, where I am drawn to a commotion. Someone is holding a child over the water, submerging her face. Everyone tells me that he is saving her, but I can see that she cannot breathe. I struggle out of my boat, run and grab her from him, her small body heaving and vomiting water. I awake and stare into the blackness, my heart beating.

In the morning my dream still clings to me. I linger in my warm sleeping bag puzzling over the image of the child's face submerged, struggling to grasp something still lying under sleep's surface. Suddenly I remember the way Anne died. She was working with another woman on a puffin colony on the north side of the island. That afternoon, they went about their measurements of burrows in their usual silent companionship. They had been out of sight of each other for some time when Anne's co-worker decided to check in with her. She walked to where she had been working, calling her name. Anne didn't answer. After a short search she found her. She had fallen only about twenty-five feet from a rocky cliff, but she had come to rest unconscious and face-down in a tide pool.

I think of my own daughter at home and am reminded with a quick sear of pain, that Anne was someone's child.

I unzip my bag and sit hunched for a while in the small space between my bunk and the one above, trying to shed the images of death. Finally, I reach for my clothes and pull them on. I have been wearing them for three days. They are rumpled. My jeans have grass and guano stains on the knees.

In the kitchen Laura and Richard are already up, brewing tea. I tell them about my dream. They share similarly frightening dreams. There is something disturbing about Triangle to every one of us here. Perhaps it is more than Anne's death. Perhaps this place was never meant to be inhabited. Not since the last people were taken from the ill-fated lighthouse in 1922 has anybody attempted to live here year round.

I take my bowl of yogurt and granola out to the porch in front of the cabin, and sit on a driftwood bench. The wind that tore the roofs off the lightkeepers' houses and drove smoke down chimneys is nowhere to be seen today; Triangle Island is coy. Her skirts of golden grass fall in long pleats to the shore, fringed with a border of fireweed gone to seed. Planted among them, the sign with Anne's name on it stares implacably to sea. I lean back in the warm sun, stretching my legs out where once we spread our skirts and toasted the puffins' arrival.

August 23

I close my sketchbook and a small watercolour set filled with my favourite hues: aureolin yellow, cobalt blue, alizarin crimson, viridian…Today I had hoped to paint Puffin Rock, but it is elusive, impossible to capture its complex cracks and contours, the light playing on its skin of green and gold. Frustrated, I put down my brush and set off for a walk.

The tide is out. The rocks are draped in glistening seaweed. I pick my way among the beach cobbles, squinting at the ochre shadows folded into the cliffs of Puffin Rock. Painting has taught me to look for the colour in every shadow. I look down at the stones at my feet. To my surprise, one moves. I crouch—a Cassin's auklet chick presses itself into the ground. It is about the size of my hand, sleek and pale grey, with a few last wisps of down on its rump. A tiny white crescent over each eye gives it a surprised look. It must have tried to fledge last night, under the safe cover of darkness; this was as far as it got. It will be hours before the tide comes in. The journey to water, where the bird can dive to safety, is a long one in the perilous light of day.

This bird is strong and healthy. Cassin's auklets are having better luck feeding their chicks this summer than puffins. Its wings beat against my hands as I scoop it up. I carry it over slippery kelp to the water's edge, where I open my fingers and it flutters out, leaving a warm dropping in my palm. It paddles off erratically, then orients like a compass needle and begins swimming to sea.

August 25

I have fallen quickly into the rhythm of the days on Triangle: waking, eating, working, sleeping. Research leaves little time or energy for anything else. There is a sense of urgency as the short season nears its end. We are carrying out studies designed by biologists who are not here with us. In the winter they will analyze our data. It must be complete or it will have to be discarded, and the summer wasted.

Only at the end of the day, coming home from the colonies, do I dawdle. I walk slowly, searching for nothing, looking at everything. I find a bird skeleton, a tiny corset of white rib bones, suspended from reptilian vertebrae, and an empty chiton shell, curled up like the hand of a sleeping child. I turn it over to find the beautiful turquoise enamel underneath, usually hidden by the flesh of the living animal. I thread my way among tossed-up logs, spotting plastic bottles and floats, yellow and blue polypropylene ropes, torn fragments of driftnet. A lace emerges from sand. I tug at it, dig and unearth a tattered running shoe. It is a white high-top, about my size, with the black Nike "swoosh" logo. I brush it off, set in on a log and look beyond it to the western horizon, empty save for a line of clouds flying like white spinnakers. I note a familiar slipping between what I feel and what I know: I feel a world away from everywhere; I know the earth has been gathered tight in invisible nets of shipping lanes, flight paths, radio waves, fibre optics. The shoe was made in Korea. Bound for the shopping malls of North America, it rode an ocean to get here.

I remember the story of these shoes from newspaper articles when people first began picking them up on beaches. In 1990 the container vessel *Hansa Carrier* was en route from Korea to the US Pacific Northwest, heavy with close to a thousand railroad-car-sized containers, packed with everything from VCRs to perfume. About 1,400 nautical miles off the West Coast it was hit by a severe late spring storm.

Five of the containers that toppled off the *Hansa Carrier* were jammed with a total of 80,000 Nike shoes. Six months later, thousands of running and hiking shoes began washing up on western beaches. Even after a year in the ocean many of the shoes

Part Two

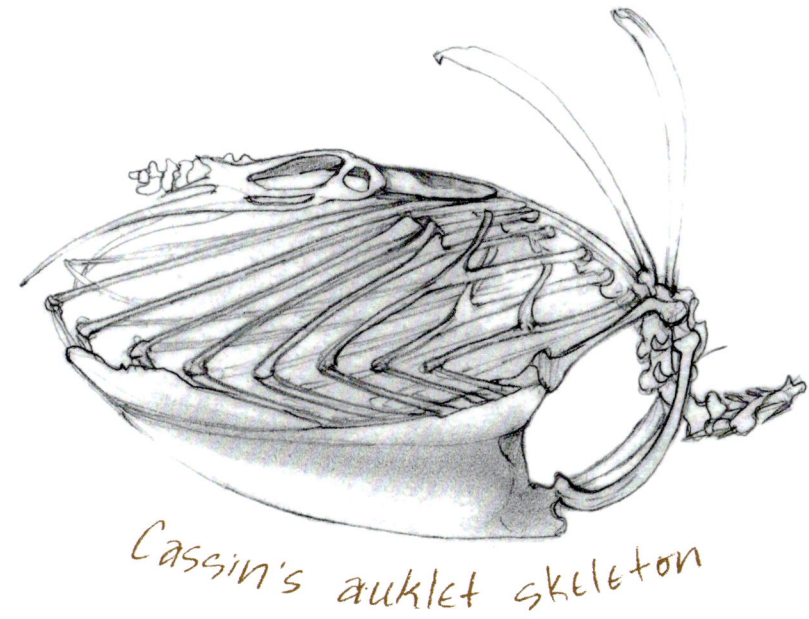

Cassin's auklet skeleton

were wearable, once the barnacles were scraped off them and they were washed. Unfortunately for beachcombers, they weren't tied together. People formed exchange networks, and held "Nike Nights" and swap meets to find matching shoes. The project became a media event. National papers published the story, urging the public to contact them about shoe finds.

Scientists seized this "spill of opportunity" to study the tracks of the empty shoes across the Pacific. An instantaneous release of possibly 80,000 drifting "markers" was a boon to the study of ocean currents. The scientists calculated that the shoes travelled a simple path, due east on the Subarctic Current, then dispersed over 600 miles of coastline, carried by seasonal currents that follow the continent's shores. They were thrown up on the wild beaches of the Queen Charlottes in the winter; dropped on Oregon's curving sands in June. About two years after the spill, running shoes were found on the northern end of the Big Island of Hawaii. They had been caught in the southward flowing California Current, then travelled west. Scientists predicted that, if the shoes lasted a few more years, they would boomerang back to Asia.

A few years later blue turtles, yellow ducks, red beavers, and green frogs began showing up on western beaches. Having escaped from their steel ark when a container ship bound for Tacoma from Hong Kong met a winter storm, they were ideally suited for their ocean journey. They bobbed along for almost a year before reaching land, a cheerful flotilla of almost 29,000 plastic bath toys, in the world's biggest bathtub.

Their first landfalls were near Sitka, in southeast Alaska. Though their spill was farther out, they drifted past the Nike site. Then, still far at sea, they took a northeast turn, and eventually sailed into the Gulf of Alaska. Their course diverged from the Nikes, partly because of annual differences in currents, but also because they were light and rode higher—they were caught by the wind. Oceanographers predicted that some of the toys would continue north, slip through the Bering Strait into the Arctic Ocean, to Siberia with the Arctic pack ice, and eventually reach the North Atlantic Ocean. Such blithe messengers to bear the sober reminder of how small our world is; that it has always been connected: by current, by winds bearing rain evaporated from distant seas, by seabirds threading the globe with their slender flight.

Looking past the Nike stranded on this shore, I imagine what it's like to be far at sea, where the currents are born, on the puffins' wintering grounds—a gyroscopic world of water and sky, pinned down only by horizon. Below, plankton and fish move through columned light. Past the first fathoms, where long warm wavelengths no longer penetrate, the light becomes green then blue and finally flickers out in a cold world where colour has no meaning. Animals are spangled with bioluminescence, communicate and hunt with semaphores of light, call to each other in darkness etched with sunken maps of whale song.

The ocean seems complex as the cosmos—beyond unravelling. Is the puffins' hunger this season part of a "normal" cycle or a more unsettling event, a red flag for unnatural change?

The sea has always been fickle. It is normal for puffins to have difficulty feeding chicks some years. Recently, breeding tufted puffins on Triangle Island have had very low fledging rates. The effects of this are yet to be seen.

Part Two

In the last hundred years this coast has been altered in many ways. The great salmon runs, which nurtured the cultures of the people of the Northwest Coast for thousands of years, are failing, diminished through over-fishing, the destruction of countless spawning streams through logging, and the industrialization of estuaries. Recently, biologists have proposed that shifting ocean conditions due to climate change are influencing survival of salmon at sea, where they feed after leaving their streams and before returning to spawn and die.

Some research suggests that unusual ocean temperatures alter the survival rate of plankton as well as the timing of their seasonal movements in the water column. Peak zooplankton production is happening earlier. Perhaps the fish puffins depend on, particularly the mysterious sandlance, are not finding the plankton when and where they should. The sandlance may be either not surviving as well as a result, or shifting their own behaviours so that they are not where the puffins expect to find them at the time they need to feed chicks.

There's no sandlance fishery in our waters, unlike in the North Sea. The North Sea sandlance harvest (mostly for fish meal and pet food), along with the herring fishery, is probably the main reason that seabird colonies are failing there. With the collapse of salmon and the search for alternative fisheries could these waters see a sandlance fishery in the future? How will the puffins, already struggling, survive?

In 1998, the Geological Survey of Canada released an optimistic report on the possible oil and gas reserves in the waters off British Columbia. Presently there are both federal and provincial moratoria on offshore drilling. Recently the British Columbia Government Scientific Panel on Offshore Oil and Gas Development released a report in which it supports the lifting of the BC moratorium. Oiling is already a problem for our seabirds. Every year over 300 tankers ply this coast. There have been five major spills in the past 17 years. The last left about 56,000 seabirds dead off Vancouver Island and Washington. Several hundred minor spills occur each year. The inevitable spills from offshore drilling will amplify losses.

I try to think what I would say to a fisherman looking to sandlance as the only chance to continue his way of life. What could

the old steam donkey engine: 1980

1996

I say to an unemployed logger hoping for a lifting of the moratorium on this coast? How to defend puffins? Perhaps I would suggest that they can be indicators of the health of fish stocks. I might mention the unexpected ecological effects of removing sea otters from this coast and quote conservationist Aldo Leopold: "To keep every cog and wheel is the first precaution of intelligent tinkering." Could I express my deeper conviction—that the smallest, most insignificant creatures have intrinsic worth; that imagination is impoverished in a world where the value of living things is only calculated in dollars?

Protecting the Scott Islands and their surrounding waters, with their huge breeding colonies, is crucial for our seabirds. They provide that rarest of laboratories, a relatively unaltered ecosystem—free of the oil drilling, fisheries and human disturbance that have devastated seabird colonies in many other parts of the world.

More than ever before, scientists from many disciplines—ornithologists, marine biologists, oceanographers, and meteorologists—are working together to try to understand ocean changes. It's not easy.

I look out beyond the bay. The ocean is misleadingly uniform, stretching unbroken to the horizon, unchanging except for the sky's reflection and the print of wind. In fact it is in constant dialogue with air, light, heat, cold, rain and rivers. It answers with currents and counter-currents, not only on the surface but deep below, with upwellings and downwellings, and by separating into layers of different temperatures, density and saltiness. All these responses shift with the seasons and from year to year. The life histories of its plants and animals, molded by forces we can't see or measure, are often impossibly complex. Having just begun to study the ocean, it's impossible to tell which changes are short, which long term, which are normal, which potentially catastrophic. Most scientists agree that a climate change is underway. Most believe that it is linked to global warming. Will protecting these islands and their waters be enough for the birds?

I pick up the running shoe again and turn it over. Perhaps if I searched this beach I would find its mate. More likely it is still riding the great currents. Who knows what subtle changes are occurring far out at sea where it began its journey?

Part Two

August 29

On our last day the island gives us a gift—a blue sky. We decide to climb to the lighthouse. Our packs loaded with binoculars and cameras, we set out for the west side of the island. I walk along stone near the shore. Though these black rock ledges have swallowed millions of waves since I was last here, they have not changed. As I jump from one to another, I wonder if I've changed. I have the same desire to sit and stare out to sea, the same tendency to daydream. Perhaps we don't really change, but, like the sea, simply get more concentrated, parts of us evaporating off. As I search the slope above me for the pale scar of a trail I wonder where time would have taken Anne.

Above us, the eagle nest sits empty on its pinnacle, its jumble of twigs like a strange pyre. Beyond it the ridge begins its long snake to the summit.

My companions set off with fearless agility, and I fall into line behind them, gaining elevation as we pick our way along the crumbling vertebrae of rock. The ridge is several feet wide, but on either side the land drops, opening in wide folds at the shore, hundreds of feet below. Between the folds are steep gullies, eroded by millennia of rain.

Though I reassure myself that my feet are planted firmly, it's no use. My body won't listen. My legs shake uncontrollably. I feel the fear that has nested in me over the years. I was always cautious in high places when Anne and I worked here, but I can't recall this sense of terror. During all those long days climbing, sometimes alone, up and down Puffin Rock, I didn't think death could touch me. Now it has a face, unlined and framed by a halo of sun-bleached curls. This face, Anne's face, has been hovering at the back of my mind ever since my return to Triangle Island.

I think of the great tide of birds that flood here from the ocean each spring, the thousands of dead chicks on the colonies this summer—profligate birth, extravagant death.

The others stride on ahead, their colourful backpacks bobbing. I take a deep breath and continue climbing. A few minutes later, the ridge gives way to the high plateau, and we beat our way through salmonberry to the summit. The old donkey engine has collapsed into a brittle pile of rust since I was here with Anne, but otherwise the place looks much the same: house foundations slowly crumbling into the salal, the grey concrete tower a hard silhouette against the sky.

We hoist each other up onto the high, wide ledge encircling the base of the lighthouse. Each of us finds a spot along it, stretching our legs and pulling lunch out of our packs. As we pass around a Thermos of mint tea, sparrows emerge from the shrubs below. Perching on high branches in the bright sun, they throw their heads back and trill, their throat feathers parting. A shadow passes over us, and we hear a call like a stone being dropped into water: Raven, who gave light to the world.

After lunch we lean back against the tower wall and gaze out over the island, each of us lost in thought. I look up at the blunt crown of the tower above me, where the powerful light was stripped long ago, when men finally gave up on Triangle Island. Built with tremendous effort and complete confidence in technology, in the worst possible place, it was doomed to fail.

Sitting in the sunlight, I imagine the island in the months to come, abandoned like a shipwreck, the golden sea of grass turning brown, beaten by winter winds, the puffins scattered over the ocean of storms until spring. For centuries birds have gathered here, returning with simple, perfect faith, because the sun was high and they yearned for land.

I get up and walk the circle of ledge, taking in the scene below me where Triangle's emerald mantle sweeps away in long curves. In the next few weeks the puffins we have been studying this summer will leave these slopes. The season has been disastrous—for reasons all our science cannot explain, the waters did not provide for them.

Below, the sea is scaled with silver light; the tide is turning, shifting its heavy body south. To the east, Vancouver Island is suspended over a diaphanous layer of summer fog. Beyond its immense forests, nourished by sea-borne rains, lie the cities that will reclaim us soon. To the west, the empty Pacific waits for the birds.

EPILOGUE

In 1983 Anne's parents established the Anne Vallée Ecological Fund. It is awarded each year to graduate students doing field research into the problems of animal ecology in relation to human settlements and activities such as agriculture, forestry, industry, fishing and tourism. Since then it has supported the work of many students from both Quebec and British Columbia, including research on Triangle Island.

The year I returned to Triangle Island was one of the worst seasons on record for tufted puffins. In 1997 and 1998 puffins again struggled to raise healthy chicks—fewer than ten percent of the chicks in monitored burrows fledged. To the great relief of researchers, in 1999 and 2000 the fledging rate was over ninety percent. The next year started out well, but halfway through the summer chicks began losing weight. Only about half of them fledged.

A picture is beginning to emerge of a connection between water temperature and the breeding success of seabirds. Records of sea surface temperatures on this part of the coast go back to 1937. The years when sea surface temperatures are high can be correlated with low fledging years for puffins. Never have there been as many consecutive warm years as in the 1990s.

Puffins also fail when unusually cold waters sweep in, as in 1976 and 1977. However, in 1975, the coldest year, they fledged normally. Possibly there is more flexibility in food availability in cold than warm years.

This summer biologists returned to Triangle Island to continue the painstaking work of uncovering the puzzling links between ocean and birds.

mallard
wing feather
(speculum)
dropped by a male
who arrived mid-August,
stayed for a week, then left

NOTES

PART I:

April 29, 1980
The three outermost Scott Islands—Beresford, Sartine, and Triangle—are ecological reserves, managed by British Columbia Parks, access to which requires a permit and is limited to researchers. Combined with the two innermost islands—Lanz and Cox—they form Scott Islands Provincial Park.

May 5
The story of the Triangle Island light is told in detail in *Keepers of the Light* (Graham, Don. Madeira Park: Harbour Publishing, 1985).

The lantern from Triangle light was brought back and reassembled in Victoria and can still be seen at the Canada Coast Guard base at Ogden Point.

May 8
When Ferdinand Magellan arrived in the unknown waters to the west of Cape Horn, in 1521, he had just endured a stormy Atlantic winter in southern Argentina. Hitting an unusual patch of good weather, he crossed the uncharted ocean in steady, pleasant winds. Because of this he named it "Pacifico," Spanish for "peaceful." He did not know that this body of water was vast enough to hold all the continents, with room left over for an extra Asia, or that the Pacific, especially at high latitudes, whips up some of the worst storms on earth.

May 10
The great auk was a swift and agile swimmer but clumsy and vulnerable on land. Mariners herded the birds from their breeding colonies on offshore islands right across gangplanks and onto boats. Slaughtered at first for their meat, their feathers became valuable. Their eggs were collected and their chicks used for fish food. They disappeared from Britain around 1760. This may have been partly because of the "Little Ice Age," which began around the thirteenth century and lasted until the end of the nineteenth, surrounding their colonies with ice, giving polar bears access to them, and perhaps changing fish populations.

May 18
The micro-organisms that should be present in some of the rocks of Triangle Island are radiolarians and diatoms, deposited over millions of years in the Jurassic and Cretaceous periods. The bodies of these types of organisms make up a majority of ocean sediments.

May 29

The name "Kwakiutl" arose as a misunderstanding among the Europeans who settled the coast. The Kwakiutl are only the people who lived at what is now known as Fort Rupert. It is more correct to refer to the people speaking the Kwak'wala language (of whom the Kwakiutl, or Kwagiulth, are a tribe) as the Kwakwaka'wakw.

The Yutlinuk were closely associated with the people who lived on the very northern end of Vancouver Island, the Nahwitti Tribes of the Kwakwaka'wakw.

The story of Siwidi and a photograph of the otter mask can be found in the book *Chiefly Feasts, the Enduring Kwakiutl Potlatch* (Jonaitis, Aldona, ed. Vancouver: Douglas and McIntyre, 1991).

Cook's visit to Nootka Sound is described in *Captain James Cook, a Biography* (Hough, Richard. New York: W.W. Norton & Company, 1994).

The first appearance of the name Triangle Island was on the charts of a Spanish expedition (schooners *Sutil* and *Mexicana* in 1792), where it is labeled "Isla Triángulo."

The Russian Bering Expedition to the North Pacific in 1741 brought back sea otter skins and introduced them to China, trading for, among other things, tea. The Chinese quickly came to prize the fine pelts. The Russians returned to the Aleutians, virtually enslaving the Aleuts, proficient otter hunters. When the animals were depleted there, they brought Aleuts south to Sitka, the new capital of the Russian American Company.

As the sea otter became rare, trade shifted to land furs, trading posts were established and traditional lands were under pressure by colonists. Decades of commerce with Europeans changed the economic and political relationships between West Coast tribes. Diseases such as small pox decimated villages, leaving them vulnerable to intertribal warring raids. Some villages were abandoned completely as groups who had lived apart amalgamated, often on the much reduced territories of newly designated reserves.

Potlatches were outlawed in the early part of the last century. They continued in secrecy until they became legal again in 1951.

June 2

The story of the cannibal from Triangle Island appears in *Kwakiutl Tales* (Boas, Franz. New York: Columbia University Press, 1910).

June 3

The only furred animals on Triangle Island are mice, voles, rabbits descended from lightkeepers' stock, and the sea lions that breed on offshore islets.

June 10

Change can sweep through the small isolated populations of islands, creating new, specialized forms—a process known as "genetic drift"—more quickly than on large land masses, where new genes are quickly diluted in a continuous "gene pool."

June 22

Though the moon is much smaller than the sun, because it is closer to the earth it exerts greater force on our waters. At a full or new moon, the earth, moon, and sun are in alignment and the moon's effects are slightly amplified by that of the sun. These are called spring tides. At the solstices the position of the earth in relation to the sun intensifies the sun's effects on the earth, creating the year's greatest tides.

The science of mapping the moon, or selenography (named after Selene, the goddess of the moon) was founded by Johannes Hevelius, a wealthy Polish brewer, in the seventeenth century. His nomenclature was replaced by a system published in 1651 by Giovanni Battista Riccioli. This Jesuit astronomer named, among other things, the seas that can be seen by the naked eye.

The largest of the seas or "maria" is the Mare Procellarium or Ocean of Storms, lying on the moon's western curve. Ornithologists place the seabirds that ride the winds of the stormiest oceans—albatrosses, fulmars, shearwaters, and petrels—in the order Procellariformes.

Bioluminescence is commonly created in northwest waters by large blooms of a type of phytoplankton, called dinoflagellates (the same organisms that produce red tide). The term phosphorescence is often applied incorrectly to the light dinoflagellates produce. Phosphorescent light, produced in chemical reactions that involve phosphorus, requires a prior absorption of light from an external source.

June 25

The underwater world is described in *Kwakiutl Culture as Reflected in Mythology* (Boas, Franz. New York: G.E. Stechert and Co.,1935).

July 2

Island gigantism is discussed in *Evolution of Mammals on Islands* (Nature, April 18, 1964: 234-235) by biologist Bristol Foster, who studied mammals of the coastal islands of British Columbia.

July 13

Oystercatchers are what ornithologists call "precocial," that is, hatched covered with down, legs well developed, eyes open and alert, and soon able to feed themselves.

When the tide is low, oystercatchers spend most of their time feeding. Eating about a third of their body weight every day, they can consume in a year more than a hundred pounds of mussel meat.

It was the shaman's special relationships with animals that gave him or her the power to cure pain and illness believed to be wrought by witchcraft. The dances and songs the shaman performed with drums, rattles and staffs summoned the spirits and put him into the trance in which he could communicate with the animal world. In these rituals, he took on the spirit of the animal he invoked. It was thought that, privately, shamans could take the form of animals. Accounts of shamanism describe the shaman as achieving a state of ecstasy in order to fly between three levels of the universe: earth, air, and water. To summon flight, shamans dressed themselves in feathers, wore bird masks, and shook rattles carved in the shape of oystercatchers.

July 15
Petrel reference: Matt. 14:30. (King James Version)

July 19
With small, stiff wings, common murres are reputed to be the most agile divers of the alcids. One reference claims they have been tracked in waters over 150 feet deep. But with such large bodies, any more wing concessions in favour of aquatic agility would soon render murres flightless.

Fossils of birds who live and die mostly at sea are rare. Some 50-million-year-old fossils of primitive Pacific auks have been found. But the present distribution of the auks is our main clue to their origin. Alcids have radiated dramatically in the north Pacific. Of the eighteen species here, sixteen are endemic, that is, found nowhere else in the world. There are only four endemic alcids in the North Atlantic. This suggests that the family evolved first in the Pacific. When the Bering Strait was open between ice ages a puffin predecessor winged its way into the Atlantic. When the strait closed, the birds were cut off and developed in isolation into the common or Atlantic puffin, the puffin we know best as the icon on everything from postcards to coffee cups. In the Pacific this first puffin evolved into two closely related species: the rhinoceros auklet and the tufted puffin. When the strait reopened, the Atlantic puffin slipped back into the Pacific. By this time it was too different to interbreed successfully with the other puffins here and it evolved into our final species of puffin, the horned puffin.

August 1
Dr. John Ford discovered and first recorded the differences in dialects among BC's killer whales.

Graeme Ellis has studied BC's killer whales for more than thirty years. He reports that the northern resident pod currently consists of about 200 animals, while the southern has 80.

August 10
The capacity of a puffin to excrete salt is among the highest rates known in birds. Theoretically this capacity would not be needed by a fish-eating bird (as fish body fluids are less salty than seawater). M.P. Harris, in his book *The Puffin* (London: T. & A.D. Poyser Ltd., 1984), suggests this evolved to rid the birds of salt swallowed in sea water during winter, when they feed more on plankton.

August 20
Just where puffins go in the winter is a mystery. Radio tagging and tracking is costly. Boat surveys can be difficult in rough winter weather. Marine transects (survey lines along which observations are made) are simply too few and far between to reveal where the majority of birds are.

Other observations of puffins in the Atlantic wintering from the southern edge of the arctic ice pack to the Azores could mean that the birds are scattered, with two or three every square mile.

In the 1980s the West Coast Offshore Exploration and Assessment Panel recommended that inventories of seabirds be taken to establish "normal" or baseline information. Ornithologists hitched rides on research vessels involved in other oceanographic work. In about ten years they plied over 12,400 miles of ocean, counting birds every ten minutes along over 5,000 transects, stopping only for heavy rain, fog or rough weather. Only 1,000 miles of ocean was surveyed in winter but those counts showed that, after November, puffins weren't anywhere to be found on or near the continental shelf.

PART II:

August 25, 1996

This wasn't the first time small floating objects had been used to learn about currents. Between 1956 and 1971, three major oceanographic programs released about 200,000 drift bottles in the eastern Pacific.

Conservation of this part of the coast has been proposed. The Canadian Wildlife Service has consistently stressed the importance of a Marine Protected Area, with a minimum six-mile zone around the Scott Islands. It has recently begun the Scott Group Marine Assessment for the purpose of defining an appropriate area under the Canada Wildlife Act. The CWS hopes to establish the first Marine Wildlife Area specifically for marine bird foraging. Other groups such as the World Wildlife Fund and the Canadian Parks and Wilderness Society would like to see the Cook Bank to the north included, as it is very likely an important feeding area for seabirds.

The moratorium on offshore oil exploration and drilling is both provincial and federal. Both levels of government must approve its lifting. The BC Government Scientific Panel on Offshore Oil and Gas Development supports the lifting of a moratorium, although it concedes that "significant gaps remain in a number of scientific and technical areas that would be of special relevance to British Columbia if the government should decide to…consider programs of offshore exploration and development." The panel stresses the need for marine ecosystem research and better oil spill response and notes the decline in scientific expertise and monitoring capacity in both BC and federal agencies, stating that "at present there is insufficient capacity for the research, assessment, monitoring and management needed to provide an adequate baseline knowledge framework for ocean and coastal policy-making."

SELECTED BIBLIOGRAPHY

Campbell, R. Wayne et al. *The Birds of British Columbia*. 4 vols. Victoria: Royal British Columbia Museum (vols.1 & II); Vancouver: UBC Press (vols. III & IV), 1990, 1997, 2001.

Cannings, Richard and Sydney Cannings. *British Columbia: A Natural History*. Vancouver: Douglas & McIntyre, 1996.

Carl, G. Clifford, C.J. Guiguet, and George A. Hardy. *Biology of The Scott Island Group, British Columbia: Report of the Provincial Museum*. Victoria: British Columbia Provincial Museum, 1951. pp 21–63.

Ebbesmeyer, Curtis C. and W. James Ingraham, Jr. *Shoe spill in the north Pacific*. Eos, Transactions, American Geophysical Union, vol. 73, no. 34 (August 25, 1992): 361–365.

Ehrlich, Paul R., David S. Dobkin, and Darryl Wheye. *The Birder's Handbook: A Field Guide to the Natural History of North American Birds*. New York: Simon & Schuster Inc., 1988.

Eiseley, Loren. *The Immense Journey*. New York: Vintage Books, 1946.

Ford, John K.B. and Graeme M. Ellis. *Transients: Mammal-Hunting Killer Whales*. Vancouver: UBC Press, 1999.

Galois, Robert. *Kwakwaka'wakw Settlements 1775–1920: A Geographical Analysis and Gazetteer*. Vancouver: UBC Press, 1994.

Graham, Donald. *Keepers of the Light*. Madeira Park: Harbour Publishing, 1985.

Haley, Delphine, Ed. *Seabirds of Eastern Pacific and Arctic Waters*. Seattle: Pacific Search Press, 1984.

Harris, M.P. *The Puffin*. Calton: T. & A.D. Poyser Ltd., 1984.

Harrison, P. *Seabirds: An Identification Guide*. Boston: Houghton Mifflin Co., 1983.

Hendrickson, Robert. *The Ocean Almanac*. New York: Doubleday, 1984.

Hough, Richard. *Captain James Cook, a Biography*. New York: W.W. Norton & Company, 1994.

Selected Bibliography

Hoyt, Eric. *The Whales of Canada*. Camden East: Camden House Publishing, 1984.

Jonaitis, Aldona, ed. *Chiefly Feasts: The Enduring Kwakiutl Potlatch*. New York: American Museum of Natural History, 1991.

Kozloff, Eugene N. *Seashore Life of the Northern Pacific Coast*. Vancouver: Douglas & McIntyre, 1973.

Lockley, R.M. *Puffins*. London: J.M. Dent & Sons Ltd., 1953.

Murray, John A., ed. *A Thousand Leagues of Blue: The Sierra Club Book of The Pacific*. San Francisco: Sierra Club Books, 1993.

Nelson, Bryan. *Seabirds: Their Biology and Ecology*. New York: A & W Publishers Inc., 1979.

Obee, Bruce and Graeme Ellis. *Guardians of the Whales: The Quest to Study Whales in the Wild*. Vancouver: Whitecap Books, 1992.

Payne, Roger. *Among Whales*. New York: Dell Publishing, 1995.

Pojar, Jim and Andy MacKinnon, eds. *Plants of Coastal British Columbia: Including Washington, Oregon & Alaska*. Vancouver: Lone Pine Publishing, 1994.

Reid, Bill and Richard Bringhurst. *Raven Steals the Light*. Vancouver: Douglas & McIntyre, 1984.

Richards, Alan. *Seabirds of the Northern Hemisphere*. New York: Gallery Books, 1990.

Ricketts, Edward R. and Jack Calvin. *Between Pacific Tides*. 4th ed. Stanford: Stanford University Press, 1968.

Rodway, M.S., M.J.F. Lemon and K.R. Summers. *British Columbia Seabird Colony Inventory: Report #4 – Scott Islands*. Delta: Minister of Environment Canadian Wildlife Service, 1990.

Schultz, Stewart T. *The Northwest Coast: A Natural History*. Portland: Timber Press, 1990.

Strauch, J.G., Jr. *The Phylogeny of the Alcidae*. The Auk 102 (July 1985): 520–539.

Thomson, Richard E. *Oceanography of the British Columbia Coast: Can. Spec. Publ. Fish. Aquat. Sci. 56*. Ottawa: Minister of Supply and Services, 1981.

Turner, Nancy. *Food Plants of British Columbia Indians: Part 1/ Coastal Peoples*. Victoria: British Columbia Provincial Museum, 1975.

Vermeer, K. *Nesting requirements, food, and breeding distribution of rhinoceros auklets, Cerorhinca monocerata, and tufted puffins, Lunda cirrhata*. Ardea, 67 (1979): 101–110.

—-. and L. Cullen. *Growth of rhinoceros auklets and tufted puffins, Triangle Island, British Columbia*. Ardea 67 (1979): 22–27.

—-., Ken Summers, and Daniel S. Bingham. *Birds Observed at Triangle Island, British Columbia, 1974 and 1975.* The Murrelet 57 (Fall 1976): 35–42.

Wehle, D.H.S. *The food, feeding, and development of young tufted and horned puffins in Alaska.* Condor 85 (1983): 427–442.

Welty, Joel Carl. *The Life of Birds.* 2nd ed. Philadelphia: W.B. Saunders and Company, 1975.

ACKNOWLEDGEMENTS

I am grateful above all for the unfailing support of my husband, Kim Waterman, and our children, Lindsay and Sophie, who have had to share me with this project for many years.

I am also profoundly indebted to Isabelle Gutmanis, from whom I learned much about the craft of writing. Writing friends from whom I have received inspiration include: Kelley Aitken, Nancy Baron, Maria Coffey, Carol Matthews, Anna King, Robert and Kit Pepper-Smith, and the Nanaimo Women's Writing group.

Others who offered help and support include Trudy Chatwin, Jane MacRae, Mike Hawkes, Francis Sprout, Mark Kaarremaa, Malcolm Watt, Thora Howell, Bob Bossin, and Terry Jacks. Thanks also to Brian Falconer and Erin Nyhan of Maple Leaf Adventures.

I am grateful to the Banff Centre for the Arts where I attended the Writing Studio and was fortunate to work with editors Rachel Wyatt and Edna Alford. The Canada Council generously provided a travel grant.

Thanks extended back through the years to Dr. David Shackleton and Steve Short, and more recently to seabird researchers: Anna King (who appears as "Hannah" in the manuscript), Laura Cowen, Richard Leland, Jeremy Kendal and Suzanne Romain, for excellent companionship and cooking.

Seabird research on Triangle Island occurs under the direction of the Canadian Wildlife Service and Simon Fraser University's Chair of Wildlife Ecology. Thanks also to BC Parks for their careful stewardship of this precious place.

In the course of writing *The Last Island* I have sought out many experts. Their passion for seabirds has been inspirational, their generosity and expertise invaluable. They include ornithologists Dr. Doug Bertram of the Canadian Wildlife Service and the Simon Fraser University Centre for Wildlife Ecology, who gave me the opportunity to return to Triangle Island and spent hours answering questions; Moira Lemon and Ken Morgan of CWS; Colleen Cassady St. Clair of the University of Alberta, and Carina Gjerdrum.

For insight into the fauna and currents of the Pacific I am indebted to Peter Olesiuk from the Department of Fisheries and Oceans; Ron Tanasichuk; Bruce Lehman of the Pacific Halibut Commission; Richard Thomson and Bill Crawford of the Federal Institute of Ocean Sciences in Sidney; and Curtis C. Ebbesmeyer of Seattle.

More indispensable information was furnished by geologists Jim Haggart of the Geological Survey and Kristin Rohr; historian Dick Wells; ethnologist Martha Black of the BC Provincial Museum; Keith Symington of Canadian Parks and Wilderness Society and Stephen Hume of the *Vancouver Sun*.

Finally, this book is indebted to Anne Vallée, adventurous spirit and promising ornithologist, whose tragic loss is still difficult to believe and whose absence will always be felt by those who knew her.

INDEX

Bold type indicates illustration

A
abalone, 153
albatross, black-footed, 73–75
alcids, 40–41. *See also* auk, great; auklets; common murres; penguins; pigeon guillemots; puffins
Aleutian Low, 36–37
Anderson, W.P., 30, 34
anemones, 97, **98–99**
Anne Vallée Ecological Reserve, 12
auk, great, 40
auklets: Cassin's, 22–23, 80–82, 85, 128, **130**, 145, 147, 165, **167**; rhinoceros, 117, 120–121, **122**, **130**, 132

B
barnacles: larvae, 78; 100
Biggs, Mike, 142
bioluminescence. *See* oceans: bioluminescence
Boas, Franz, 68
Boston, 148
Brunton, Miss, 33–34

C
Canadian Wildlife Service, 12, 23
Cassin's auklets. *See* auklets: Cassin's
chiton, 96, 166
columbine, red, **95**
common murres: description, 67; wings, 75; nests, 78, **126**, **130**; colonies, 125–126, **127**, **138–139**; diet, 128

constellations. *See* stars
Cook, James, 60–61. *See also* *Discovery*, Nootka, Nootka Sound, *Resolution*
cormorants, pelagic, 23, 123–125, **130**
cow parsnip, 87, 92
crabs: larvae, 78; hermit, 97
currents. *See* ocean: currents

D
Darwin, 92–93
Davies family, 32–33
Discovery, 61
DNA, 163
Duff, Wilson, 60

E
eagles, 84–88
Eiseley, Loren, 91
Elliott, Sidney, 33–34

F
Faeroes, 43
falcons, peregrine, 113
ferns, 28
fireweed, **118–119**
fishermen, 64–69; names for seabirds, 73–74
fog, 121, 123
fur trade, 61, 63

G

Galiano, 33–34
gap. *See* Puffin Rock: gap
geology: volcanoes, 51–53; Wrangellia, 52; California trench, 52; Queen Charlotte fault, 52; Pacific plate, 52–53; earthquakes, 52–53; Triangle Island, 53. *See also* Mount St. Helens
gigantism. *See* mice
glass balls, Japanese, 96
Graham, Donald, 30
great auk. *See* auk, great
gulls: and kleptoparasitism, 44–45, 129, **138–139**; nests, 78; chicks, **131**

H

halibut, Pacific, 65, 66–67
Hansa Carrier, 166–167
hermit crabs. *See* crabs: hermit
Home Bay, **8**, **16**
hummingbirds, rufous, 89, 91–92

K

kelp, 63; bull, **143**
killer whales. *See* orcas
Kwakiutl (Kwakwa̱ka'wakw): territory, 59–60; Yutlinuk, 59–60; and sea otters, 60; versus Nootka, 61; *hamatsa* dances, 68; and sea lions, 104–105; and orcas, 142–143; and ravens, 153–154; and sky, 155

L

Lanz Island, 60, 109
larvae, marine invertebrate, 78
Leopold, Aldo, 172
lesser yellowlegs, 146
lily, chocolate, **94**

M

Maquinna, Chief, 48
Mariner's Weather Log, 36–37
Martin, Mungo, 59
mice, 93, 108–109, **110**
monkey flower, 89, **89**
moon, 101. *See also* ocean: tides
Mount St. Helens, 51–52
mussels, 96

N

Native peoples, West Coast: preparing ferns, 28; calling fair winds, 37; Greenland Inuit, 43; and shells, 56, 59; and mice, 111; Tlingit, 123, 124; and seals, 161. *See also* Kwakiutl; Maquinna, Chief; Nootka
Neary, Jack, 33–34
Neary, Michael, 33–34
Nootka (Nu-chah-nulth): meeting James Cook, 61; versus Kwakiutl, 61
Nootka Sound, 61, 63
North Bay, **8**, 67

O

ocean: waves, 57; currents, 77, 167–168; layers, 77–78; tides, 101; bioluminescence, 101; as drinking water, 148–149; temperature, 169; changes, 172
oil, 169
orcas, 140–143
oystercatchers, 56–57, **58**, 116, 117

P

Pacific High, 36
pelagic cormorants. *See* cormorants, pelagic
penguins, 40–41
peregrine falcons. *See* falcons, peregrine
petrel, 123
pigeon guillemots, 78, **79**, 80, **130**
plankton, 75, 77, 78, 132, 169

Puffin Rock: **8**, **22–23**; hiking, 20, 21–22; nests, 47–48; gap, 67–68, **86**, 116

puffins: nesting, 21, 22, 41, 44, **50**, 80, 82–83, **130**; arrival, 27, 38–41; as alcids, 40–41; description, 40, 43; social behaviour, 41, 44; flying, 41, 43; predators, 41, 109, 111, 113; edibility, 41, 43; protection, 43; mating, 43–44; migration, 44; lifespan, 44, 140; and gulls, 44–45; Atlantic, 44–45, 82, 132; burrows, **42**, 45, 47; droppings, 45; at sea, 65, 68; incubation, 82; eggs, 83; hatching, 112, **114**; chicks, 112–113, 135, **135**, 136–137, 140, 162–163; horned, 128; fishing, **45**, 128, 129, 131–133 **134**; drinking seawater, 148–149; fledging, 149, **150**, 151; survival, 168–169. *See also* research methods: puffins

R

rats, 109–111
ravens, 124, 153–154
research methods: puffins, 45, 47–48, 82–83, 112, 113, 129, 131–132, 133, 135, 136, 143–144, 149, 162–163; Cassin's auklets, 80–81
Resolution, 61
rhinoceros auklets. *See* auklets: rhinoceros
Ricketts, Ed, 97, 100, 153
rockfish, black, 105, 108
rookeries. *See* sea lions: rookeries

S

sandlance, **122**, 132–133, 169
sandpipers, western, 145
saxifrage, **91**
scallops, 100
Scammon, Charles, 141
Scott Islands, 9, 21, 59, 92–93, 109. *See also* Lanz Island

sculpins, 97, 100, **103**
sea anemones. *See* anemones
sea lions: and rookeries, **8**, **46**, 104; Steller's, 67, 104–105, **106–107**, 115
sea otters: in Kwakiutl legend, 60; as food, 61; and fur trade, 63; diet, 63; re-establishment on Triangle Island, 63
sea stars, **71**, 96, **98–99**, 102
sea urchins. *See* urchins
seals, 140–141, 161
shearwaters, 73
shells, 56, 59. *See also* abalone; Native peoples: and shells; whelks
silverweed, 88–89, **90**
snails, 100
sparrows, song, **81**, 92
sponges, **98–99**, 100
star fish. *See* sea stars
stars, 155
steam donkey engine, 30, **170–171**
Steinbeck, John, 100

T

thrush, Swainson's, 144
Triangle Island: **8**, **10**; 1980 trailer, **8**, **16**, 17, **39**, **86**; 1996 cabin, 12; dangers, 13, 30–34; BC's largest seabird colony, 20; lighthouse, 21, 29–30, **31**, 32–34, **86**, 174; skeleton, 30–31; wireless/telegraph station, 32–34; weather, 36–37, 121, 123; geology, 53; outhouse, 57, 59, **62**; soil, 59; wildflowers, 88–89; description, 93, 95. *See also* Home Bay, Kwakiutl, Native peoples, North Bay, Puffin Rock
Triangle Island Users Manual, 12
troller, 66
tufted hairgrass, 21
tunicates, 96, **98–99**
Turner, Nancy, 28

U

urchins, 63, 97, 100, **115**

V

Vallée, Anne: family, 26; studies, 37–38, 153; favourite music, 49, 54; Quebec politics, 49–50; **135**, **150**; description, 154; death, 160, 164, 173. *See also* Anne Vallée Ecological Reserve, research methods

W

water, drinking, 147–148. *See also* ocean: as drinking water

Watt, Alison: family, 26, 27; childhood, 48; and death of puffin chick, 136–137; and death of Anne, 164, 173. *See also* research methods

waves. *See* ocean: waves

whales: minke, 69; humpback, 69, 72; fin, 69–70, 72; grey, 72. *See also* orcas

whelks, 56

worms, 100

Y

Yuquot. *See* Nootka Sound

Yutlinuk. *See* Kwakiutl